# Come
# Live
# Love
## *Guidance for Life*

**EMMANUEL LORD**
AS TOLD TO SHARON SUE HILLER

ISBN 979-8-88851-522-8 (Paperback)
ISBN 979-8-88851-523-5 (Digital)

Copyright © 2023 Emmanuel Lord
All rights reserved
First Edition

All rights reserved. No part of this publication may be reproduced, distributed, or transmitted in any form or by any means, including photocopying, recording, or other electronic or mechanical methods without the prior written permission of the publisher. For permission requests, solicit the publisher via the address below.

Covenant Books
11661 Hwy 707
Murrells Inlet, SC 29576
www.covenantbooks.com

# *Preface*

I have desired to put together a book for all people everywhere that will live on and make a difference for the future of mankind. They seem to need pulling back. There is too much isolation and not enough caring in some places. Other people are still moving forward just like I intended, but with all the electronics and social media, things seem to get lost.

I write about things that you may not know. I am everlasting, and so is My word. I have shared some of the hidden things that will help you to live a better life. I want to help you in all that you do. What is important is that you come to Me.

I have shared these words with My servant, Sharon, who has written them down by listening to My voice. You, too, can hear My voice if you listen to your heart and get quiet. Be still and know that I am God.

So much of the words that My people have shared through the centuries are true. I have always been and always will be. I have led people to share My thoughts. Many of the things recorded in My Word show the things that have happened through the years. What I want you to remember is that I am constantly with you, drawing you to Me. I will not come uninvited. Oh, that you would invite Me to come to you and that you would come to Me.

As you read, please understand My deep love for all of creation. Draw near and hear what I have to say. Then listen for yourself and know that what I say is true. I want the best life for you always. It is My hope that these thoughts will be helpful and start an awakening of love around the world.

Emmanuel Lord

# Contents

| | |
|---|---|
| Take Time | 1 |
| Questions for Self-Reflection | 2 |
| Beginning | 4 |
| Creating the World | 5 |
| Man and Woman | 7 |
| Brotherhood | 9 |
| Creativity | 11 |
| Colors Are Unique | 14 |
| Uniqueness | 16 |
| Peace from God | 19 |
| Prayer and Trust | 21 |
| The Call | 23 |
| Plans | 24 |
| Turning Life Around | 25 |
| Get to Know Me | 27 |
| Three in One | 28 |
| Observations | 31 |
| Addiction | 33 |
| Transformation | 35 |
| Simplify Food | 36 |
| Healing | 38 |
| Healing of the Mind | 40 |
| Life Issues | 42 |
| Obedience | 44 |
| What Breaks God's Heart | 46 |
| Live Life | 48 |
| Love Others | 49 |
| I Wait | 51 |

| | |
|---|---|
| Live Life to the Fullest | 53 |
| Come to Me | 54 |
| Love from the Heart | 56 |
| Take Hold of Peace | 58 |
| Holy Spirit | 60 |
| Life | 61 |
| Light | 63 |
| Prayer Direction | 65 |
| Worship | 68 |
| The Gift | 70 |
| Warriors of Love | 71 |
| Church, Arise | 73 |
| Wave of the Spirit | 75 |
| God's Love | 77 |
| Love and Prayer | 78 |
| Doing God's Will | 80 |
| Heal the Earth | 82 |
| Food | 83 |
| Color | 86 |
| Balm of the Spirit | 87 |
| God's Word Is True | 88 |
| Life Within | 89 |
| Peace from the Heart | 90 |
| Giftings | 92 |
| Love the Earth | 94 |
| God's Intention for Life | 96 |
| Care of the Earth | 98 |
| Man's Direction | 99 |
| Rest and Unity | 101 |
| Taking Action When Called | 103 |
| Love Everywhere | 105 |
| Love and the Fruit of the Spirit | 107 |
| The Gift of Peace | 109 |
| New Day | 111 |
| Choose Well | 113 |
| Listening | 114 |

| | |
|---|---|
| Prayer | 116 |
| State of the World | 118 |
| End Times | 119 |
| Created for Relationship | 120 |
| Lifestyle | 122 |
| Lament | 124 |
| Remember | 126 |
| Earth | 128 |
| Barriers | 130 |
| Relationship to God and Others | 132 |
| Sacrifice and Love | 134 |
| What God Has Done | 136 |
| Trust | 138 |
| Love Overflow | 140 |
| Love in Abundance | 141 |
| Blood | 143 |
| Commands | 145 |
| Glory on the Earth | 147 |
| Stillness | 148 |
| Give Your Cares to God | 150 |
| Love Always and Everywhere | 152 |
| Light and Love | 154 |
| Honor God | 156 |
| What Is Love? | 158 |
| The Light Shines Within | 161 |
| Darkness to Light | 163 |
| Dwell in the Light and Truth | 165 |
| Our Example | 167 |
| Let Love Grow | 169 |
| Love Heals | 172 |
| Imitate Me | 174 |
| Openness | 175 |
| Pearl of Great Price | 177 |
| Praise Me | 178 |
| Truth | 180 |
| Joy | 182 |

This Is the Day ..................................................................... 183
Joy in Each Day ................................................................... 185
Seek God's Words ................................................................ 187
Joy Comes ........................................................................... 189
Joy Explodes ....................................................................... 190

## *Take Time*

The life that you live now could be so much better.
Thinking and dreaming of things to come won't make it happen.
It's the things that are from the heart that really matter
So live in the quiet places from within and you will see
That the soul that is placed there holds the key to your identity.
Your life is but a moment here and then it's swept away
To a place that I call home for all eternity.
You can make each moment count and there is much to share
If you share what's on your heart and take some time to care.
I have placed My people here to grow in certain ways
Because I know connection is the thing that needs to raise
The soul within to greater heights that will allow the praise
Of all the beauty that is shown in everything I birth
And the glories of creation all around the earth.
Please take some time to discover the light you have within
And let it penetrate your life and free your heart from sin.
You are such a precious child and I need your help each day.
I want to send the children love in all you do and say.
So please take time to shine your light and help to show the way
For someone else to look inside and share the light, I pray.

## *Questions for Self-Reflection*

Have you ever thought about your life? Is it a life that you enjoy living? How do you spend your time? What are the activities you find easy? What are the activities you find difficult? What is the most satisfying thing you have done in the last two weeks?

Who are your friends? How did those friendships develop? Are they satisfying? What do you contribute to those friendships? Is there someone you wish you could have as a friend? What are the qualities that draw you to them? Do you see those qualities in your own life?

What is your relationship to God? Do you pray? How often do you pray? What do you and God talk about? Do you listen to Him? What is He telling you? Are you following Him with what He is asking of you? Do you read the Bible? Is anything jumping off the page to touch your heart? Are you being obedient to His word?

Are you taking care of yourself? Do you know what that even means? When you are alone, are you comfortable with yourself? Do you try to find ways to distract yourself from being alone? What do you tell yourself? Are you kind? Do you beat yourself up? Do you feel like there is no one you can share your heart with? Is there something you wish would stop going around in your head? Are you sleeping well at night, or are there thoughts that cause fear and lack of sleep?

Is the job you are in right now one that you enjoy? Are you doing things that help sustain your spirit? Do you feel like you are contributing to the workplace? Is there something you would like to share that might make a difference? What is stopping you from sharing it? Do you need to look for something different where you feel you can shine? Do you need to be your own boss? How do you think that would work for you? Would you be a kind boss? Would you have enough energy and motivation to keep yourself doing what is needed?

Is there a dream that has been running around in your head? Have you made any progress toward it? Could you take one small step toward it today? What will you commit to doing? Who do you need the support of to keep it going? Do you need funding or help?

When you think about the future, do you have hope or fear? What is it that causes that? Is there something you could do to gain hope over the situation? Is there a roadblock you need to move before going forward?

It is amazing that every person is so different, and yet each one needs to move forward in life. It takes much reflection to make progress and to grow. You can do it, a little at a time. Thinking about this, you can only really make one change at a time. Many people procrastinate rather than move forward. You may need help to break out of your old pattern to get to a growth mindset, but it is worth taking time to do it. When you do, you will see that it is totally worth it even if it happens slowly, which is often a way that it sticks. Don't be afraid to ask yourself the questions. Just keep moving forward toward those goals. Worthy goals are something to strive for each and every day. Think about these as the big "first things first" pieces of the day. If there is time for more, then do it.

# *Beginning*

In the beginning of time before the world began, I was there in the universe before there was anything created. I dreamed of a land where there were other thoughts and voices. There was only one. Then there were two and then three. We formed a family. We are the Godhead, three in one, for we all came from the same being as we divided in sacrifice to make another.

I will never regret the sacrifice to have another One to connect with. It was a joy. The three of us could look in different directions and plan together. Our communication was in thought. Our minds spoke to one another. We had no other language. It was the language of love. It was pure. It was kind.

Because we are light, we created other lights. The galaxy is made up of the light that we sent out into space. These lights broke off into other lights. Because of their gravitational pull, those lights that sparked off revolved in a circle around it. Some lights went out and became a big mass.

These masses were cold on the outside and still burning inside. I found that there were some of the burned-out stars that could support life. I had a fun time making the earth. It was able to support lots of different life. We decided to use our creativity on earth. That is why you see so many different colors, shapes, and sizes there. It was fun to use our creativity to make fish, flowers, trees, food, animals, birds, and a variety of men and women. Nothing was the same. All life was unique.

The people were given the responsibility for caring for the earth. They chose to do their own thing rather than care for what I made. It makes Me sad, but I have hope for the future. I know that there is a new vision for the earth.

# Creating the World

In the beginning when I created the world, I wanted to fill it with love. The little creatures were fun too. I enjoyed playing with the cells and seeing how they fit together much like people put Legos together today. Finding ways to group cells and helping them to be filled with My light and love was fun. I enjoy being creative. I changed the colors and the shapes of things. These living, breathing things became My life. I was infatuated with them.

I started with the plant life after separating the waters and the land. I knew that whatever I created would need a way to have sustenance. The plants grew. They became food for My first animal creatures. I put energy into everything that I made, energy that could allow the living things to grow. I experimented with different types of seeds, making them just a little different each time. They were unique. Even when I put the same thing into the seed, the plants grew a little differently. I wanted them to be able to reproduce, so I helped this by making the plants to create seeds. This is the wonder. I needed to create in each seed the way for it to grow and reproduce so it could multiply on the earth. I put the seeds in the earth and watched them grow. I put some in the water, and they also grew. This provided food for the creatures that I had in mind.

Starting with little cells, I created things that breathed on their own. Each cell had intelligence to know how to grow and reproduce. The more cells that I put together, the more they had variety. They grew bigger and bigger. These fish as they came to be called were given seeds within them to reproduce. I created them male and female so they could be together. I made them in like ways as male and female but allowed them to come together to reproduce. My idea was that they could live together and make more like I did with the plants. The water animals thrived and continued to grow.

As I made the land animals, some could go into water and also survive on land. It was fun to continue to make bigger and bigger creatures. Each one had intelligence to know how to eat and reproduce. Some had more brains than others. They learned how to survive. They learned which animals might be for food. It was like a fight to see who was the strongest. Oh, yes, it was interesting to see who won out. The weak didn't survive. The strong did. They kept growing and changing. I enjoyed the various creatures that I made. I tried all different colors and shapes. They were fun to create. Some made it for many years. Others didn't adapt well to where I placed them, and they died out. There are many creatures that didn't live. Through the years, many more died out.

Yes, hunting other animals for food is an innate thing. All the living things need food. All the living things need water. All the living things need to reproduce in order for our world to continue. When I created the birds of the air, I had the most fun. Starting with the littlest ones, I knew that they would fly. I wanted to have them bigger, but then I needed to have a way for them to reproduce. It was fun to make male and female look a little differently. I created strong wings that would help them to fly. They ate the seeds from the plants that were on the land. They survived in the plants when they rested. The trees held their nests so they could lay eggs. These creatures have a brain that helps them to survive. They go where they can get food. They fly long distances. Sometimes they travel together.

The animals found shelter in the tall grasses, in the trees, under the ground, in caves, and in places that supported them. The animals adapted to the place where I put them, or they died out. They often roamed out of the place I created for them. Some had tough skin. Some had layers of fat to keep them warm. Some were bright colors. Some were very tall; others were low to the ground. This variety allowed all to be able to have different food and survive in the same environment. They ate the food from the trees and fields. They also ate the meat from each other. It was all good.

# Man and Woman

When I created man and woman, I put My Spirit within them. It was very good. I wanted to have conversation with them. I wanted them to love Me. I wanted them to be able to care for the earth so I could move on to other projects. It was beautiful in the beginning. I had a beautiful garden for them to live in. They didn't live long before they disobeyed and ate of the tree that I asked them not to eat. I knew that it would be a bad thing for them because it was giving them feelings of not being enough. Yet they ate the fruit. Their disobedience was something that caused Me great anger. I didn't want them to eat it, and they did it anyway. I told them they could have so many other things, but they weren't satisfied. Since I really didn't want them to eat the tree of life and live forever, I took them away from that place, and I destroyed the original plan.

I so wanted to have love in return for the love that I gave humans. I thought that since I made them in My image, I could get reciprocal love, but there wasn't any way that they could do that if they couldn't follow what I asked. I allowed them to live, but as they reproduced and went on in life, more and more of the people continued in a way that was so contrary to what I wanted. I was furious. I decided to destroy the earth and start over.

I didn't really want to have to start completely over because I had spent so much time creating things. That's why I chose Noah and his family to build the ark and save many of My creations. I knew that the land animals wouldn't be able to survive the water, so I covered the earth and started over. It grieved Me to know that I spoiled My work, but I couldn't see another way.

After the flood, man started over, and so did the animals. The plants slowly came back, for their seeds in the earth were able to withstand water. Some didn't come back as I had hoped, but there were enough that it made a good climate for the animals.

Man is difficult. When I created him like Me, I didn't realize that his choices would make a downturn. The good man and his offspring eventually became corrupt as well. It was sad to see. The people didn't pay Me much attention. They wanted to do their own thing. They wanted to set themselves up as God. I couldn't handle that. It made Me so sad. When people didn't share their love with Me and went their own way, I was very discouraged. I let them continue because I made them. Man destroyed so much of the earth by the way he lived. The thoughts and intents of his heart were no longer pure. He went off on his own, trying to build his own empire.

Still there are some who come to Me, some who take time to listen to Me, some who honor Me, and some who love Me and love others. There is still good in the world. I want people to concentrate on the ways that I have set to love Me and to love others. Will the world ever come back to that kind of love? I know that in the end, there will be love. There will be honor. There will be glory. My people, who are called by My name, will humble themselves and come to talk with Me as I designed them to be. Then I will restore the land to the way that I designed it to be. I will love them, and they will love Me. It will take time.

Those who do not want to honor Me will be burned in the lake of fire. I will have no use for them. This is My final judgment. I desire to have all come to Me. Will you help them be saved from the judgment? Come. Let us go into the world together and save mankind from sin, hatred, and evil ways. This world is worth saving. Come unto Me, and I will give you rest. Be at peace, not war. Join together in love. That is My design. Can you bring it together? It will take everyone working together for it to be completed well. Yes, I use the good and the bad to create My perfect ways. Remember it takes all of creation to make the world the best place it can be. Don't just consider man but all things. Don't be selfish. I made the whole world, and all of it is precious to Me. Let it be.

# *Brotherhood*

Do you realize that all people came from one man, Adam? Eve was created from Adam's rib. Together, they populated the earth with their children's children. The generations have been going on for thousands of years. Multiplication is the result of the seed that started from the Maker's hand. All things that were made were meant to multiply and fill the earth.

People began in a central place and walked out from there. They chose to explore, to have more space, and they just kept procreating. When people lived very long lives, they had quite a line of children. Often the oldest children were married and going out on their own when the youngest came into the world. The generations were merging. The time for children was still relatively short compared to the long time that people lived.

As people lived closer to the equator, their skin tone was baked by the sun. This caused the pigments to change over time. Those who lived in the north and in the south had lighter skin since they were further from the equator. Facial features over time were changed depending on the foods that were eaten. The people all were created to be unique. They were a blend of parents and a touch of new creation. People who carried their children on their backs had a different structure to their faces. Squinting in the bright sun caused eyes to be more closed. Adaptations had to happen due to environment.

Mankind is one big family. Tracing back through the generations, it all makes sense. However, man has chosen to look at differences rather than on similarities. I created all people with a soul. That is what lasts forever. The soul within each person knows that there is a brotherhood of man that draws all men together.

Why do men continue to look on the color of skin, the opening of the eyes, the breadth of the jaw, the features of the face? Why can't men look at the heart? That is how I see the people, with their hearts. It is what is in the heart that shows the worth of a man. It is in sharing the love that I placed within each heart that brotherhood is made. Can you look within and see the way of God is to have one race? The human race is really all that matters. As you look for what is the same and see people for the good within them, the peace of Christ will rule your hearts. Only then will true brotherhood be possible. Join together in unity and be as I intended. It will make all the difference.

# *Creativity*

Creativity is My joy. I started by creating the world. It was a joy to see how I spoke and it came into being. I delighted in each step of creation. I love the variety that was created. Step by step I learned how to put together life giving forces that would procreate themselves to last for a long time. I had to choose the perfect spot in the universe for the world to be able to have the climate it needed for each of the plants and animals that were created. It is amazing how the revolving of the world gave rise to the perfect way for night and day. The seasons work well in some areas. The heat was perfect for others. The cold required a bit more creativity. But as I contemplated and tried new things, I saw how I had to adapt.

I know that I have placed creativity in each person as part of being created in My image. I have given people a mind to think, to speak, to hear, to ponder, to pray, and to communicate with Me. I have given people the ability to work, to create, to build, and to help others. I have allowed people to come together just like many of the animal groups. However, they have the ability to learn, to grow in their minds and hearts, and even to change their thinking as they learn more. They really have abilities of all the animals and more because of My Spirit that was placed within them.

Creating things is so much a part of man. Inventions have come in many respects, and that is why there is a newer way all the time. I know that the simple ways are best, but the complex really get My attention because I started simple and moved into more complicated, creative endeavors. Man was My crowning creation.

I really wish that all people would use the creative nature I have placed within them. Art is one way to have that happen. Invention is another. Caring for others is a way that takes creative thought.

Surprises come when people are using their creative mind. They create interest and joy for the receiver as well as the giver.

When people use their creative minds, they are generally more relaxed and happier. It gives them an outlet for the mind that I put within them. It allows the brain to light up in new ways. It stimulates the heart and mind connection. It gives new life to the cells. It revitalizes the whole body. Why wouldn't people seek to activate this from within? It has so many life-giving characteristics.

Some creative things become useful. That is when they are called inventions. They carry a purpose that more than one person finds helpful for living. This might be using plants, rocks and minerals, metals, soil, or other natural resources in a new way. It might help health, comfort, work, home, or life. People have earned money with these inventions.

Artwork is something that is often created for one's own pleasure. When someone else admires it and desires to put in near them, it can also be a productive income. Much of art is just for one's own enjoyment and pleasure. It is something that takes practice, just like all things that are new. Some people have a great flair for making artwork that is beautiful.

Music is a blend of melody and harmony. It also has a creative way about it as people express their opinion, beliefs, and hopes through music. Some music lifts the spirit. Some expresses emotion. Some is for celebration. Some is calming. All music is creativity put into notes and rhythms. It is self-expression. It can touch the very soul and spirit. It is helpful to calm or excite. Through the years, so much music has been created. It is soothing to My soul. It is often healing to the bones and the inward parts if people would take time to listen and absorb its message.

Drama has helped many people to come to an understanding of life. Sometimes it just entertains, but often there is a message that penetrates. Acting things out often helps people through situations. Comedy helps the body heal through laughter. I do not like comedy that is hurtful to people, but good clean fun is a blessing to the heart. Laughter does so much for the body and mind. Oh, how I wish My people could laugh especially at themselves. A good laugh each day can do more than you can imagine.

Whenever you can, take time to tap into the creativity that I gave you. It will be a river of life to you.

## *Colors Are Unique*

Step into the world of color! I created color and have used it to give variety to all the species of plants and animals, My living things. I have allowed some colors to be brilliant and others to blend in.

Think about the wonderful palette of color that you see around you. There are shades of color in the rocks, in the leaves on the trees, the bark on the trees, in the flowers, in the vegetables, and in all of the plants you eat or enjoy seeing. As you look at the birds, there are reds, oranges, blues, yellows, greens, browns, blacks, and every shade of color. Some are mixed colors of a beautiful blend in their feathers. Think about the animals even on a farm—the pinks, browns, blacks, reds, grays, etc. I have so many different colorings to make them unique. Every animal has a unique shape and coloring. The animals in various parts of the world are colored uniquely to protect them or make them stand out.

People have different coloring. They have learned to use the colors that I made to color their clothing and to color the material objects they have around them. Things that are mass-produced are often the same, but things that are creative are always different, one of a kind. I made things uniquely and delight that people take time to make things uniquely.

Colors can help you to see things more vividly. When there is color, there is interest. Your eyes are drawn to blues like the sky and greens like the trees and the grass. Having too much color is often hard on the eyes, so a variety makes a good blend. I know that the eyes can pick up much more vivid color than you see on earth. It is a dimension that is for another time.

People choose favorite colors due to how they feel when they are around them. Certain colors look pleasing to people. They are drawn to the color because of their inner being. I know that the people feel restful and peaceful around certain colors. Others make them feel alive and energetic. What people need, they place around them.

Blending of colors creates an array of beauty. Keep looking for colors that intrigue you. Some blends are so unique that only I could make them. You can blend pigments, but to keep them going from generation to generation is something only I can do. You can enjoy the colors I have made because I gave you eyes to see. May your eyes enjoy the feast of color! May your spirit rejoice!

# *Uniqueness*

Have you ever thought about what it is that makes you unique? I have placed a different set of characteristics in each person. I don't do carbon copies like the manufacturers do. My work of creation is a one-of-a-kind plan. I am an artist with variations for each of My creations. I love to mix it up.

Think about the variety of colors I have placed on people's skin. I have allowed mixtures of pigment to blend through the years with intermarriages. I love each color. I love each shape. I love the blending of colors with hair, eyes, and skin.

I placed different gifts within each individual. They need to spend time discovering what those are. I gave each person something special that will allow them to make their mark in the world that will also help others. I planned for people to live in community. Within each community, I placed a variety of gifts. That is so they can be self-sustaining and keep the community in good health. As people move around, they still need to find a way to use those gifts to help others. Often when I move someone, it is because a community is missing what they have to offer.

I have allowed the basic body to be the same with a few tweaks. The body systems work the same. They aren't always in the very same place, but they are similar. Sometimes when the child is growing in the womb, some changes occur. It might be due to the way they move around. It might be just the way the cells grow at a rate that wasn't expected. Each body even in the womb is knitted together with unique characteristics. It is more than just the DNA that makes a person. The mother's feelings and health have a big impact on the child while in the womb. Many of those things are innate carried from the ancestors. Yes, it happens that grandparents have an effect on their grandchildren from the beginning. All of life is intertwined. The seed is passed from generation to generation.

I have allowed people to think. Their brains are able to hold so much information that is new. However, I placed a good deal of information that runs automatically into the brain so that all systems will work automatically. It takes no work on the person's part to do these automatic things. However, there are times when there is a blockage that happens of a changing of cell membranes through blows to the head or chemical changes that injure the brain. When that happens, the automatic systems are hampered from doing their job properly. This is when there is disease. People may need help to complete the work.

You have many things that happen automatically. When there are issues with feelings, the chemicals within cause there to be a disturbance. I am able to help you through these things, but these are signals that tell you that help is needed. You can calm the signals through prayer. Sometimes you can be active to jolt them out. Whatever happens, these must be dealt with in order to get them taken care of. Pushing down chemicals or calming them through food or drink is not healthy. You must deal with them now or later. Now is a much healthier approach.

I have made brains that are creative and some that are very rule-minded. They both can help others. Some people are precise, like seeing the world in black and white. Others have a lot more gray. Each person is filled with the gifts to make the world work together. Every mind has some good and some bad that must be worked through. It is available to take in things it sees and hears. Minds become a product of their own environment. They adapt well to changes and love to change and grow.

People don't always want to change. They become comfortable in the place they are living, working, and doing. When they don't change, they get left behind because the world around them is always changing. That is why I built in adaptation. It is needed in order for people to be able to live in this world.

Changes aren't always for the better. Sometimes changes cause issues because some people drag their feet. Others don't think that it is good. They perceive that this would go against what I would want for the world. At times, they are right. In this case, they need to suggest another way to make changes that would be more positive.

The human body is a great thing because it has My spirit within. It is created in My image with many abilities that other animals and plants don't have. Take time to use your brains and spirits. Don't just go through life on automatic. Make a contribution to the world in which you live. You were created uniquely for such a purpose. Use it well.

## *Peace from God*

Take time to live fully. Take time to love. That is why you have been created. I desire for you to spread My love to others. I have given you love for that purpose, so remember to share it every day. As you share it, it will be replenished. Try Me and see that what I say is true.

I have promised to be with you always. That doesn't mean once in a while. It means always. I have placed My Spirit within My creation. I expect for you to access it and use it for good. It is amazing to Me how many people have chosen to disregard My gift. I know that there may be reasons, but none of them make sense to Me. Why wouldn't you open a gift and use it?

I had a great plan when I created man. He was to take care of the earth. He was to be one that had the Spirit to connect with Us. He was to be Our presence in the world that was multiplied for good. Sin spoiled the original intent. Unfortunately, sin spread, and the love that was to be so great was diminished. This love is still available to all. It must be felt and nurtured. It must be given away in order to be multiplied. That is My plan. May man get the right idea and begin to make the love within transfer back to the world and its people as intended.

The peace that comes from knowing and trusting Me is also a needed commodity in this world. So many people are stressed doing things without asking Me for direction. I can give peace, but people are choosing to ignore My presence. I can't bring peace if people don't come to Me to receive it. This is causing them to feel more stressed. To relieve stress, they hurt themselves and others because their emotional health is not in balance.

Finding balance can only come when people take time away with Me. Some people are choosing to meditate. Others are exercising. Others are seeing therapists. Don't you realize that I am the Counselor? I can help carry burdens and bring you rest. I can forgive sins. I can bring understanding. I can provide the peace that passes all understanding. I am the answer to all of your problems. I walk with you through them and allow you to be healed and peaceful.

Did you realize that there are so many people who are walking around desiring to have what I can give? I need your hands and feet, your voice, your heart. It is the only way to reach people who have become insensitive to My spirit.

I implore you to come to Me! Come! Come! Bring others with you! Allow My heart to touch you and those who come with you. Only I can bring true rest for your souls. I am the way, the truth, and the life. I live, and therefore, you will also live.

I know there are many others who are claiming that they have the way to bring peace. They will never achieve lasting peace. Only I can do that. There is a way that people have chosen to counterfeit the things that I have created, but they are all missing something. It is not the way that I have chosen.

Come to Me all who are laden with heavy burdens and I will give rest for your souls. I only am the way. Trust Me to provide what you need. Dig deep within your soul and seek what I have placed within you. It is a hidden treasure. Those who find it will rejoice. Will you seek Me within your soul?

# *Prayer and Trust*

Prayer is communication with Me. It should be as easy as communicating with people you love. I don't need fancy language. I just need honest communication from your heart to Mine. I delight in hearing from My children.

I find that too often people choose not to communicate with Me because they are afraid that I will do something awful to them. I don't cause bad things to happen. When fear wells up inside people, that causes issues that I can't easily solve because their minds get off on the fear and negative tangent. I desire to have My children talk with Me in truth. It is how we can share the best way.

When people tell the truth, it allows them to see what is actually going on. We can be talking the same language. I am truth. I know what it is and know the recesses of your mind that hold it. Sometimes it is hard to see the whole truth because of other situations that have jaded the truth in your mind. You see only a glimpse, while I see the whole. It is hard to recognize when you are masking things because your brain sees all things positive and negative. When Satan or others tell you half-truths, you often believe them. Then the truth is defiled and continues to live within you until you cast it out as falsehood.

There are times when you throw out the truth because of the lies that you have believed. It sometimes seems more real than the truth. However, if you take the thoughts and really bring them to Me, you can shed My light on it and know the truth. I am truth. I know the truth, and you don't always see it until you talk with Me.

You often make up things to stretch the truth or to make what is in your mind or heart appear true. You tell yourself things that are untrue to make an action appear to be all right. When you bring all things to Me, you will know the correct action to take. It may not be what was in your mind. However, when you bring it to Me, I know what will work the best.

Doing My will for you, and not your own, is the best way forward. It doesn't take long to hear what I have to say if you are used to coming to Me. When you learn to trust Me and keep the line of communication open, we can connect quickly. When you aren't used to communicating with Me, it takes time to know that I am there to answer your prayer request.

I desire to answer your questions and to lead you each day. I wish that all of My children would ask. It is the only way that I can lead. First, people must have the desire to know My will. Next, they need to request My help. There is nothing that I can't do. Sometimes it takes time to get the right people on board to help with the task, but I know who and where and what and why it must be done. I know that you are often in need of help. Trust Me.

I have placed in each person different skills, needs, and desires. I want them to use them to complete My work on earth. Each person has a gift to be used to help others in completing the work of love and justice. Each person can do their part. Seek Me. I know what part is to be played. Ask. Seek. Knock. Know what I have in mind for you. Then do it. It will make a difference in the world.

# The Call

It is a good day for taking stock on life. Remember Whose you are. Remember where you have come from. Remember where you are going. Do you need to make some changes?

It is always a difficult thing to make changes. However, they are necessary. How will you ever reach your dreams or make the changes necessary to move forward with love and grace?

I know that there is much on your heart that needs to be cared for. There is an abundance of love that needs to be shared. There are people waiting to help you, to make connections with you, and it all takes time. Are you willing to give it the time that it needs?

I wait for you to be willing to do what I have in mind. It seems you get scared and chicken out at the last minute. I want to use you, but I need your cooperation to do so. There has to be a good way to get there. It will require you to put aside your own will and to pick up Mine.

I have so many ways that I could use you. However, there is one way that only you can do. Will you accept the responsibility? I need you!

When there is a crisis, where do you go? How do you respond? Are you open to what My will is in that situation? Can you change your schedule to go where I need you? There is nothing more important. Will you join Me for this task?

## *Plans*

The days go by quickly. People are so caught up in doing what they have planned. What if I have a different plan? What if the plan that you are doing is not the way that I would have you to go? Take time and listen to what I have in mind. It is not always the same as what you feel like doing. My ways are higher than your ways. My thoughts are higher than your thoughts. I see the way that things will play out. I can make course corrections when people listen to Me. I am here to help you. Will you listen?

My desire is that all people would seek Me. Put Me first. As you do, all other things will fall into place. This is the first and greatest commandment. Will you let Me lead?

I know there are leaders in governments all around the world. I would love to help them like I helped the people of Israel when they turned and asked Me to do so. I helped the prophets as well when they wanted help. Will you ask for My help and turn your trust to Me?

The way forward is to let Me show you the bigger picture. You have such a limited scope. I know the hearts of all men. I alone can make the difference that really matters. When I have all of My people on board, there can be great leaps. I desire to have people caring for Me first. Then they will know they have worth and that they are loved. As they give Me their hurts, I will heal them. I know that most people today have experienced hurts that have left scars on their minds and hearts as well as their bodies. I have come to heal and make right the wrongs. Some things can't be erased, but there can be peace around those situations for I was there with you. I walk through each situation with My children. I know that there is a blessing and truth that comes forth as we examine life together. It is in those times that healing comes.

## *Turning Life Around*

The days are getting darker as information is increased.
People losing touch with others, not caring about peace.
I take My finger and place it on the map.
Wherever I place it in the world, I see a trap
Of people doing things that don't bring peace.
I am hoping one day that wars and hate will cease.

Just like the kings of old, the cry of love is past
Until you see the light that brings you hope at last.
I cry out for the kind of world I hoped that I would grow
But all around Me there is nothing that I know.
Be strong, O mighty warrior, for there is nothing on your side.
Just stand and wait for the tide to turn and change your life inside.

There is nothing more inviting than a blessing you can find
By doing simple things that are loving, caring, and kind.
So put away the hate and let your life begin
To show the person that you are from oh so deep within.
I try to hear your voice that scurries here and there
But I just keep awaiting that someone will be there
To help and guide your lives into something that is new.
I wonder each day if I will hear from you.

Take a look at what will be if you are by My side.
I have come out to greet you rather than to hide.
There is so much that is unknown, the information grows too quickly.
I want to grasp it if I can but sometimes it goes by completely.

## EMMANUEL LORD

Lord, sit with me for a while so I can get to know you
For I have felt so all alone and want to know what's true.
Please help me to understand the many words I see
And take some time to share Your life with someone just like me.

# Get to Know Me

How little you really know about Me! You have spent so little time with Me in comparison with all the other things that occupy your time. If I am to be your director and friend, I will need more of your time.

How can I lead you if you do not come to Me? How can I put My words into you if you do not listen? How can you be My hands and feet in the world without My direction? How can I change the world without your help?

I need men and women to reach out to one another in love. The way that people speak to one another matters. So often they are not speaking and not caring. They are not helping each other to have their needs met. There are people in isolation. No one reaches to them, and they feel rejected. Everyone needs some kind of connection. In order to be healed, they need a connection to Me. Will you lead them My way?

I am patient, kind, and able to create things anew. I need cooperation from people to make new things happen. I need your permission to go ahead to make changes in you. Are you willing?

I am able to do all things. Stay by Me and you will not be disappointed. Get to know My will and My ways. You will continue to be amazed!

# *Three in One*

The days are cold and dreary. Darkness falls on the earth, but I am the light within the darkness. I am Jesus Christ. I walk with you and talk with those who will listen to My still, small voice. I am the Alpha and Omega—beginning and the end. I alone know the end from the beginning, so we start.

It is time for all people to come to know Me. I am the Son of the Father. I came to earth long ago and gave My life for the sins of the world. I did My best to lead by example. Some listened. Most did not. However, I did the work that My Father sent Me to do. It was a work of personal sacrifice. It was a work of building relationships with people. It was a healing work. It was a work that helped people know they were out of line and needed to soften their ways. Some listened. Some rejected the way that I led.

The most important thing I was trying to share was love. The Father's love is so great. He is love. His love created and thought up all that is. His love reaches everywhere. Its magnitude is limitless. It is a blanket over all of creation. Some accept it. Many do not.

When I came into the world, it was different than the world in which you live because things were simpler. There weren't as many machines. Travel was slower by foot or on an animal. People took days to get from place to place. Now the world seems smaller with the transportation that is available. However, the Holy Spirit can get anywhere quickly because He is already in everything that was made. He is right there with each person alive. He spreads Himself out into all things. His light lives within each person.

There are people who have passed on to another world. Their spirit is still in both worlds. They are there to help you. There are angels to protect people, angels who are there for support. There are many things that don't really resonate with people.

I am the epitome of the light. I walk in the Father's light as do all His children. I desire to allow His light to radiate. As people take up their cross and follow Me, there are trails of light.

To know Me is to love Me and to walk with Me. There are those who walk in the light and others who choose to remain in darkness. What do you think? Which one are you? Can you see the light?

Choose to walk with Me and talk with Me. I am the way, the truth, and the life. I give you the light of life. When people are with Me, there is no darkness, only light even in the night.

In order to learn, you will need to sit at My feet. You will be at rest and relaxation. This will open you up to the words that I share.

Untangle your life. Think good thoughts. Know that I am there to help you to grow and change. Do not think poorly about yourself, your neighbor, or your friend.

In the beginning, there was not anything besides My Father. I am a part of Him as is the Holy Spirit. We are all blended together, yet we have different tasks just like people do here today in a family. We support one another and don't really work alone. Our duties are totally intertwined. I am the One who came to earth. The Holy Spirit is the One who lives within. The Father is the source of all good. He has made each of us to be love.

As the Father and I are One, we are also separate beings working together for the good of all God's children. There is an understanding that the world will not grasp until they see us face-to-face to know how we fit together yet have separate parts. I became human, but that is not My natural form. I use that form to identify with humans. I am really God.

Trusting in Me is what really will guide your life. It is hard to trust someone you can't see. It takes faith. Faith is the evidence of what is hoped for, yet it is not fully seen. It is the way to the Father as well as to Me.

The Holy Spirit is everywhere in all things. It is important to remember that even though the Spirit lives in You, He can also remind you of the things that I say. He doesn't speak on his own. He is always with you. Don't chase him away with your unbelief and by saying things that are against Him. Keep Him content with your life and your prayers.

Be still at least part of the day. Think on Me. Allow My peace to soak into your life. My peace is not like the world gives. It remains in the midst of trouble. It grounds you when you feel attacked. It brings courage to speak in a calm manner. It is so good. It is an amazing way to bring peace to your whole body, mind, and spirit. It opens you up to hear from Me.

## *Observations*

The world has been in constant turmoil since the beginning of time. That is because people have preferred their own way rather than Mine. I made man to have the ability to make decisions. I had hoped that man would want to follow Me, to listen to Me, to have Me lead them.

When the cunning tempter came to man and man decided to follow him rather than Me, trouble began. People preferred to be feeding their own egos rather than following Me. This has caused much strife in the world. It has pitted people and nations against one another. This was not in My plan. Yet I chose to make man with the ability to choose. Oh, that they would choose Me and allow Me to love them.

I am grateful that some people chose to believe Me. I have made a covenant with mankind to never destroy the earth. It has been difficult to get people moving forward to preserve the earth. Most people just want to take and not give back. This is causing harm to the earth. It may cause it to wear out and not be able to support the natural things that I created. Already there are things disappearing. I am concerned that the rate of decay may hasten.

It has been My observation of man that he seeks to be like Me in creativity. What I hope is that he will slow to a pace that is tolerable for him. The high pace is not good for him. The people are struggling to make a way for progress to happen. They are pushing and pushing causing the body to overwork. They are no longer working physically as much, but their constant push for more is wreaking havoc with their bodies. I know that I made the body to withstand a lot of physical work, but the mental work is draining because it requires so much more thought process. The body needs rest, and so does the mind. People are not taking breaks. They are working through lunch hours. They are working into the night. They take their work home. This destroys the plan that I have for rest and for family time. I look to balance the work, sleep, and rest. Stay in My plan.

I created the world to love Me and to be in communion with Me. I set up commandments that were intended to show what was important. When I came, I simplified the law into two commands that really summarize them. To love Me with all that is within you and to love others as you love yourself. Do people today love themselves? I don't think many do. I am grateful for those who love Me. I appreciate their time and their devotion. I want to have communion with My people. I want them to feel content and empowered to do My will. I want them to listen to what I have to say. There are few that do this. I want people to just be still. People are doing, going, and forgetting about being. I want to have them be with Me.

I desire to have conversation. I know many people talk to Me. They just don't talk with Me. That is My desire. I want to talk with My children. I want to help them with everything they do. Yet they think they can do it better themselves. They think they should look to their bosses instead of to Me. Yes, I want them to listen to their bosses. However, sometimes I have a better idea and could help direct the enterprise if someone would hear Me and speak up. Is anyone listening?

## Addiction

Addiction is just a good thing gone wrong. A little is enough, and too much causes a cycle that isn't good for your body, mind, or spirit. I like for you to enjoy what you eat or drink. It is when those things become too important that the addiction begins. It often begins very young. You have read stories and experienced how life gets affected and turned around. It sets off a whole host of other issues because it becomes too important. Nothing is meant to take the place of Me. I am to be the most important in life.

Addiction is misplaced sovereignty. It becomes like a god. It breaks the commandment "Thou shalt have no other gods before Me." It takes over life in a way that sends one reeling. That is because the balance is lost when I am not first in life. People lose their self-esteem because they have stepped away from the peace that I give when I am in first place. They feel guilt and shame which is a worse feeling than grief. They can't seem to understand what went awry. They just keep trying to make that good feeling happen inside again. It isn't going to happen until there is a repenting balance of putting Me first again.

Until I have first place, there is an emptiness in the soul that needs to be filled. People try to fill it with all kinds of earthly things—shopping, cleaning, exercising, drugs, alcohol, food, gambling, work, and many other things. Things won't get you anywhere. These are not ways to peace. Only I can fill that role. I want people to know that they are seeking Me. They don't have to do all these other things. I am the Way. I am the Way! There is no other.

People try all kind of paths to peace when they are addicted. They change from one addiction to another. Sometimes they have many going at the same time and find it difficult to juggle all the balls. In the meantime, it seems that there is a more complicated life. I came that you might have life and have it more abundantly. I know that is what you are after—an abundant life filled with good things and with peace.

You can only get there if you change your ways. You must find Me. Follow Me. I know the way to heal you. You can only receive that healing when you listen to Me and follow what I tell you to do. The longer you resist and rebel, the more problems you create for yourself.

Remember My yoke is easy and My burden is light. I don't put heaviness on you. You do that yourself by listening to lies, by trying to find your own way instead of letting Me lead. I desire for you to be healed, yet you insist on doing things your own way. Why? What good does it do? Can you see that it is tearing you up?

I repeat. It is only in following Me and doing what I say that will get you where you need to go. I am the Way. Please remember that. I will lead you into all truth. I will help you to put down the addiction. It won't be easy because you have a bent to that sin. However, if you look to Me daily and take up the cross of abstinence, you will be free.

I tell you that abstinence is the only way forward. It will provide you with peace as you put your trust in Me and keep your focus there. If you murmur and complain about leaving it behind, it will get the better of you. But if you keep your mind set on Me, you will be free.

What will you choose? Do you want to be free? Do you want to stay in bondage? It is all up to you.

# *Transformation*

You notice the springtime brings a transformation of the world. It happens a little at a time as I slowly reawaken the plants after their rest. I start with the rain to water the earth. The early flowers like crocuses bloom. The bulb flowers poke their heads up. Day by day, they grow a little stronger. Pretty soon they get buds and then flower. The daffodils, hyacinths, and tulips add beautiful color.

The trees awaken from being dormant. They begin to bud. Some flowers bring blossoms of white, light pink, yellow, or dark pink. It makes for a colorful world. The leaves begin to pop out on the trees. There are many shades of green. The sunshine and the rain bring them out.

These transformations are somewhat like what happens within you when there is transformation. I have placed within you the desires and the need to change. When it is awakened, it pops out as a thought. The thought is then considered by your mind and sometimes your heart. It is something that you ponder, and it keeps growing until you acknowledge the need for action. When you realize the need for action in order to change, it happens slowly like taking baby steps.

First, you try out the new behavior. You see how it makes you feel. If it is positive, you practice it again and again until it becomes a habit. If it doesn't go too well, you often give up until it comes up in your mind again.

Remembering that most transformations happen slowly, when it is something that would be helpful, you need to keep at it. Pick it up again and again until it seems more natural. All good things are worth waiting for. Keep asking Me for what you desire and for what you need. I provide the way.

## Simplify Food

Today man has made such a production out of the food they eat. It used to be so much simpler. Plants and animals were roasted. Fish were caught in the stream and cooked as needed. There was only a "one day at a time" plan. I know that there are a lot of choices now. People are trying to get rich and make life easier. Instead, go back to the simple way. Make your own food. Get it fresh. The farms are disappearing. Where will people get food in the future? All these cans and bottles of food are not really needed. People need to get back to simple fruits and vegetables, grains, and meats. The ways of canning and freezing are going to be gone as people move to having all prepackaged things and get sick from it. Their bodies weren't intended to have such richness or chemically made foods. Going back to one day at a time, the food will sustain you better. Consider not having all those chemicals in your body. They make it scream with pain. Go back to the natural way. It is what will sustain you.

Fruits that aren't modified genetically still taste good. Vegetables that grow naturally still give the nutrients that you need. You don't need the biggest and best of all foods. You need plants that will nourish you and provide what you need for fuel to live.

Meats are not nourishing you like they used to either. That is because they are mass-producing just to sell. It used to be that animals were raised on farms and lived off the land around them. It was lean beef. Some cows and pigs were fed grain from the land. Now they are kept in places that are way too small to really support their lives. It is just for money, no longer for sustenance. It is important to stop demanding so much meat of any kind. People are overdoing it continually. It doesn't really support the people well. There are issues that the animals are passing on to the people. What gets corrupted at one level gets passed down. Such is the issue with the genetically modified corn, then the meat, then the people. It is not healthy.

To live more pure would be My way. Consider ways that you can simplify your diet. Stop using the genetically modified foods. Stop using the canned concoctions. Allow your body to receive what it needs. Clear out the foods that cause issues. Eat the pure foods that are good. Take care to make sure that the food you eat is right for you. Look at the labels. Take out the genetically modified foods as well as the chemicals that are used to preserve food. Your body doesn't know what those are. It rejects them.

I want My people to return to a simpler time. I want them to shine again. I want them to not have disease that they are causing through their interaction with the environment. If they will only listen, I can direct them. They will be whole. Mankind will heal, and so will the world.

# *Healing*

Today is the day of healing. There is wisdom in the ages. The Lord is near. You can touch Him and be healed. God is in His holy temple. All the earth trembles. He is the Most High God. He desires to teach you and help you to be whole. It is all about redemption from sin. Come! Let the healing begin.

First, I require that you consider the things that separate us from one another. Yes, I know all things, but do you? Can you tell when you have disappointed Me by not being there when I asked you to talk with Me? I know that there aren't a lot of wake-up calls. This perspective is a little different than most. However, it is one perspective that I desire for you to have.

Consider what draws us apart. Is it money, fame, plans? I know that for many people it is busyness. People are just busy doing things that take their time. It might be tinkering in the garage, checking emails, surfing the Web, cleaning an area, or making food they don't need. Whatever it is, it needs to take second place. It isn't as important as being in My presence, listening to My voice, and following My lead. Nothing is more important than that.

I know that you may do things out of love for another, but they don't need to have the best of everything. You can get by with very little. I will never ask you to give up all the pleasures of life, but I wouldn't want them to be of upmost importance for you. Doing My will is what is most important.

I do My best work when you are open to it but not always aware of it. When your body sleeps, I allow the transformation to take place. I can signal cells to do the work that happens automatically. It is something that you can't do. I have placed cells within the body to fight off disease. I give dreams that can heal the mind. Your subconscious is an amazing system. It longs for Me. It seeks to fill the void when I am pushed down, away from your conscious mind. While many dreams are not truth, there is a movement that I can tap into that brings healing.

You don't have conscious knowledge of all the systems of the body that I put in place. They all work together for good. They keep you moving and able to sustain your life. Sometimes there are injuries and mix-ups that happen in the codes that were put into place. It causes confusion, and the cells don't do what they were intended to do. As you ask for healing, I have the capability of repairing codes. I don't do that all the time. It depends on the person's heart toward the matter. Sometimes the problem is so immense and the person is closed off to healing. Sometimes I have a greater purpose in mind.

People weren't meant to live on earth forever. I have a better place. The body wears out, but the spirit continues to grow. That is what goes on to heaven. I take all spirits with Me to a better place where I have prepared for all who love Me and are called according to My purpose.

The heavens are far above the earth. I have planned for people to go there. I come and take them there. I know My children, and they know Me. When the time comes, we meet face-to-face. The reunion is wonderful! Know that there is always a way for us to connect in spirit. Our hearts connecting from the time of conception never ends. It continues to grow as long as people are open to the Spirit and to the truth.

## Healing of the Mind

Healing of the body is more simple for Me than healing of the mind. This requires action on the person's part. It requires practice, changing of habits, and putting aside things that are not of Me. There is a force of wickedness that can corrupt a spirit. That can happen in so many subtle ways. I have given man a choice. There are times that the choice takes a person away from Me. I don't want that, but I also don't want people to feel obligated to do My will, which is why people have free will. The choices that are made can make the difference in what happens in their minds.

It grieves Me when people choose the way of the world over following Me. I do what I can to place people in their life to draw them back, but I will not force the issue because I want them to love Me for who I am, not because I demand it. Kings have demanded it in the past in order for people to live. I choose to just wait for people to determine that they want to follow Me. I send out the call in many different ways. The scriptures are written for people to see their need for Me. There are preachers who share messages. My children also talk about Me with others. There are so many books written about Me. Some are accurate. Others are not. People get conflicting information. What is important is that they draw close to Me. I don't really care how they come but that they come. I can heal their hearts and their lives when they allow Me to guide them. I desire to have people follow Me.

I desire to have people come to Me out of their love for Me. I can heal their lives and help them to make positive changes as they commit their path to Me. This is something that only I can do to help them have changed, transformed lives.

The Alcoholics Anonymous group found that the twelve steps work for them. They have those steps that work for many. However, what really makes the difference is that they let Me lead them. I can help them to see the problems they have created through their wayward spirits. I can help them see that following their addiction instead of following Me led to a bad end. When they allow Me to lead instead of the addiction, they have peace. That peace comes through practicing the presence of My Spirit within them. It is not because of all the writing they do. It is because of the time they spend with Me. They work hard to lay aside the object that caused idolatry in their lives in the first place and come to Me. That way I can heal them. That is My desire.

There is also emotional healing. This is probably the most difficult because it is a chemical reaction that helps the mind remember in a certain way. As that emotion comes up, all kinds of things are connected to it. The important thing about emotional healing is that emotions aren't reality. They are attached to real things, but they aren't the event. Feelings come and go. They don't last. Dealing with emotions is difficult because I have to have the event come up in order to put another emotion there. People suffer most with emotional pain because they can't rationalize it. It is fleeting. Emotions come from chemical reactions in the body that don't always make sense with the particular event. People need to sit with emotions and let them change. Fear is the hardest emotion because it sets up a chemical reaction that is in the fight or flight category. People don't know how to deal with it. It is often frightening. It is something they can't seem to share. I understand emotions and can heal them as you bring them to Me. Don't forget to do that regularly. Thank Me for making you alive and able to feel.

Of all things, I really want you to feel love. I am love. I desire for you to have Me inside you and let My love carry you through all of life's situations. It is what I desire above all else. Live a life of love. Love Me. Love yourself. Love others. Be at peace. I am with you.

# Life Issues

Life is filled with many trials. These situations are to teach you, not trip you up. They are sometimes easy to overcome. Other times they can be difficult. When these situations are brought to Me, I help to provide a way through them that makes you stronger in body, mind, and spirit.

Learning to trust Me for answers in the midst of trials is often difficult unless you have a strong relationship with Me. Even then it seems that the faith you are standing on gets eaten away by doubt and fear. Trusting Me and speaking of My goodness and mercy in the midst of the situation draws Me closer to you and you to Me. Stand firm on My promises to provide for you.

When there are health issues, I know the way to healing. I know whether this issue is from a physical, emotional, or spiritual cause. I know the inner workings of your body since I made it. I provide some of the knowledge of it to doctors who can be helpful. However, they only know a part of the issue, not the whole. So many doctors now specialize in one area, but it takes a whole team to put all of the pieces together. I know it all.

When there are relationship issues, I know the hearts of all those involved. I know the pain that is deep within each person. I know what you have stuffed down and what you have let go. I know the truth that lies within.

In order to heal relationships, it takes all parties involved. It may be that the people need to forgive. They may need to listen and understand. They may need to give grace and extend mercy. They may need to give more than they think they can. They may need to expand their thoughts to include others in new ways. I know what is needed. Asking Me for the way forward is always the best step for improving relationships.

When emotions are high, I want you to gain balance. There are times of sadness and times of joy. You can't always be on the mountaintop. You can't always stay in the valley. You can be more stable as you keep Me at the center. Staying close to Me brings peace. Seek peace above all emotions. Give out as much love as you can, for it is in giving that you receive.

When your spirit is lacking, pray. I can provide a stronger spiritual life. Take time to be still. It is in stillness that you can connect with the spirit I gave you within. Take time to be connected with Me. My wisdom and guidance are amazing. I can do all things. Remembering My word can help you draw closer. May your life be guided by My Holy Spirit.

## Obedience

Obedience to Me is important. People don't realize the blessing that comes from obeying or the havoc that wreaks in lives due to disobedience.

People ask Me for help. When I help and they follow My instructions, they avoid pain. I lead them in quiet ways so they don't realize that it is Me doing the leading. They forget that they asked. They take the credit. When they give Me the glory for the work, then I can bless them further. They have learned that a grateful heart has benefits.

So often people get overloaded, and they forget to relax and let Me do the work. They think that they can do it on their own. They want to prove to others that they know how. However, it is in handing it over to Me and trusting that I will do it that the blessing comes.

Trusting Me is important. I desire to spread goodness and give mercy to people. If they don't trust Me to do it, they will never have the ability to know that I am at work. They will not feel the joy of answered prayers. Trusting Me allows faith to grow and prosper within each soul.

I desire to help people achieve the desires of their heart. However, many people give up on their dreams thinking it is too hard because they think they have to do it by themselves. I can see all things and know how to work them out for good. When the desire is not met and it seems too hard to continue hoping for, this is when I can do My best work if people will finally allow Me to complete the work.

Some desires need cooperation from people. I can't complete the work if the person does all they can to counteract My work. When I give a word of direction, I need it to be done. It is perseverance with the plan I set that helps us to accomplish the work together. I give the words and help the actions when it is possible for Me to do. Often with interference on people's part, I wait a while to act again because it doesn't seem important to them anymore. That is when they end up losing the blessing of receiving the gift they said they desired. I need to wait to act again until they ask for My help.

When people disobey My instructions and seek other ways to get to their desired outcome, they are doomed to failure. They waste time and money on false claims that tell them it is the right way. However, I know the way that will work for each person. I didn't create people to be the same. The path for each person is unique. It isn't one size fits all or that one solution will work for everyone. That seems to be the problem in this world that has become so commercialized.

People have lost their sense of quiet in the world. They no longer take time to listen for My voice. If they would just be still and know that I am God, I could guide them in better ways. They would know how to move forward.

Oh, that My people would take time to put Me first in their lives. That would make all the difference in the world. Love would reign, and evil would dissipate. People would obey My command to love Me and to love others. What a wonderful world it would be!

# What Breaks God's Heart

What breaks Your heart, Lord?

I see My people going their own way. They have turned from the things I have taught them. They have broken My commands. They have chosen to make idols of wealth, possessions, and technology. They have not come to worship Me. They have become ungrateful for all that has been given to them.

The children are not receiving the word that I have asked parents to pass down and teach their children. They don't really know any different because they haven't been taught.

Women are aborting their children, not giving them a chance to live. They have to live with the pain of what they have done to commit murder. This is such a bad practice. It was not My intent for life. It grieves Me that the law of the land has said this is acceptable.

It grieves Me that people don't get along. This has happened since the beginning of time. I want people to live together in harmony. I want them to see that unity of heart is My way. Yes, all people are unique, but I planned for them to get along and look out for one another. I placed people in families and in communities so they could enjoy life together and support one another with their gifts and serve one another in love. I don't understand why people are turning to their own ways.

I see greed and pride getting in the way of people living as I intended. I see jealousy, the desire to be the best, competition, and strain of lack getting in the way. I see that people have forgotten to take care of others and to give respect to each person on earth. I see that there are people who cheat and lie their way through life.

People not only lie to others, they lie to themselves to the point that they don't recognize truth. Truth is absolute. It can't be changed.

Yet in the minds of people, the truth has been twisted, so there is no truth that all believe. Remember that I am truth. I know what is absolute. I use that as the measuring rod in the end days. It is not good that people turn from the truth and believe a lie.

How did minds get so twisted? They believe a lie and then another and another. Their minds are playing tricks on them. Instead of seeking Me, they seek mediums, cards, and other methods that believe they can foretell the truth. That is not the way that I intended. I want to be in direct communication with My children here on earth as in heaven. I desire for all to come to Me. I know that they will eventually, but those who do it early will make a way for others to find Me.

Oh, that there would be many more who would come to know Me, the one true God. It is My heart's desire that it happens. Please do what you can to spread the truth. It is the only thing that will really make a difference. Sharing the truth in love is an amazing tool to lead people back to Me. Share it often.

# Live Life

Live each life to the fullest. I am always available to help you with your life. Remember it was Me that gave you your life. I am invested in all you do with it. May you use it for My glory. May you use it with holiness and splendor of the One who created you.

Your life is a gift. It was given to you in trust that you would not waste it but use it for My kingdom. What have you done to help build the kingdom? What have you done to help others realize that they are My chosen instruments of love?

It is My privilege to help people to live. I am always pleased when My children come to Me. Some people are still thinking they only have themselves and need to be in control. That is not true. I need people to show them. Telling them has not made a difference because they are not choosing to believe it.

I need others to help spread the truth. Showing people through their life and their example is likely the best way to show others what is needed. Some people still choose to ignore My truth even when it is shared by someone.

How can you live life to the fullest ignoring your spiritual side? Man was created in the image of God who is Spirit. If man ignores the biggest part of himself, he will not be able to be true and live a full life. There will be a void that will be like a hole of emptiness. Only I can fill that hole. There is not another way to fill it.

Will you turn to Me so that I can help you live a full life? I desire to be all that you need. I promise to make sure all of your physical and emotional needs are met as well, but only I can fill your spiritual needs. Come to Me. Know My heart. Know My love. Receive the gift of a full life of love.

## Love Others

People are My crowning creation. I long to communicate with them. I rejoice in being able to help them and to answer questions when they come to Me. This love between us is real. I know that people are meant to be directed by Me. Yes, they have their own minds, but as we share together, life is better.

In order to have peace between people, there has to be an understanding of the person's mindset. People get their initial thoughts from parents and teachers. When those people have hatred or difficulty understanding how others live, it causes a misunderstanding to continue. In order to break this pattern, there must be something that causes change.

Love is the basic feeling that I have placed in hearts. As people look at others with a loving, kind heart, there is a willingness to build understanding. It is amazing what can happen when people use the fruit of love—joy, patience, kindness, gentleness, goodness, peace, self-control, and faithfulness. This fruit used in encounters with others lifts the spirit and enables love to thrive and cover over grievances.

Grievances with others can really color life black quickly. It is best for people to let them go. I intended for My world to be full of color. Vibrant. Glowing. Loving. When people hold onto grievances, it is like a poison that brings to them all kinds of ills. It destroys what I placed within them until they let it go and let love restore them to wholeness again.

Getting the difficult thoughts against others out of the body, mind, and spirit isn't done lightly. It is a work that only I can do. People need to be willing to allow it to flow out to Me. I can take the sin and the pain. I did it already on the cross. I have lived through all the hurt mankind has had. I made an exchange for you already. I can do it again and again because it is My desire that you live in peace.

The evil of the world can be overcome with My love. It takes people who are willing to go beyond the normal daily life to reach to others who are hurting. Extending love and kindness in exchange for hurt could turn the world around. Yes, there have been years of bad feelings passed down from generation to generation. However, there has also been love passed down from generation to generation.

My love is strong. My love is able to make hate melt into love. It takes perseverance. It takes continual acts of kindness. It is best done one on one. If each person could reach one other, I could be more effective. I am working behind the scenes to help My people care. I am doing My best to communicate to those who will listen. It is not going as well as I planned because people have become busy and more self-absorbed. I need people to seek Me and My purposes for them. As this happens, there will be more love in the world.

Take heed. Do what is good. Love and support others, especially those who are hurting. Live in communion with Me. I will direct your paths. You will find peace. You will lead others with rejoicing. You will change the world one person and one situation at a time.

## I Wait

Stay close to Me. I need My children to surround Me. That is the only way that I can help them live freely. I give direction. I answer their prayers. I counsel them and heal their hurts. I delight in My children's obedience and love.

The problem is My children walk away. They think they know what they should do. They feel they have all that they need. Their ego gets out of hand. They have their own ideas. Some of them are good. They become all consumed in the work they are doing, and they forget about Me. They get the feeling of control, and then they make their work their god.

My children grow up and have a false sense of security. They forget that I provide all they need. They get to the point where they have used up the resources they have gained in My presence, and they come up empty. They make money and knowledge their gods. They lose the truth of My ways and go after their own ways.

I try to draw My children back. I whisper to them. I put things in their memories through other people and the things they see. I know that I have to wait, and so I do. I wait and long for My children to come back to Me.

It grieves Me that so many times I have to watch them go through unneeded pain because they work themselves into a frenzy. Their bodies aren't meant to withstand so much pressure. They take on so much. The body breaks down. It can't handle the pressure that builds up inside. The signals get crossed and make My children sick.

Sometimes when they are sick, My children turn to Me. Sometimes they come to Me so I can heal them. Sometimes they choose to go to doctors. Some can tell what is happening. Others really can't. I know. Oh, that they would come to Me. I so long for

My children to come to Me. My heart longs for them. I must wait. So I wait…and wait.

If My children would just call out to Me, I would be there in an instant, holding them, loving them, helping them through their situation. I would rejoice. Instead, I weep for My children. I wait. I cry. I wait. Will you come?

## *Live Life to the Fullest*

I have given you all you need to live life to the fullest.
Remember that there are always things that are difficult.
Life has its twists and turns that take you to new places.
It makes life more interesting.
New ways of doing things change up a life.
Old ways can cause you to lose the wonder.
Just keep the eyes of your heart wide open.
Dream about the things that might be.
Keep your heart set on your Maker as you dream.
Allow the night to swallow up the pains
And free you to live life in the day.
Take time to talk with others daily.
Be kind and tenderhearted with them.
Understand the ways that they are going
And help them on the path.
Grow ever stronger in the gifts and talents you've been given.
Share them without pay to be a help to others.
Allow little things of kindness to brighten up each day
And find the love within your heart to share along the way.

## Come to Me

Come unto Me, all who are weary, and I will give you rest. Come, sit with Me. Let Me calm your fears and wipe away your tears. I am so happy to spend time with My children. Come! Let Me see you. Let Me hold you close. Come! Allow your life to be close to Mine. There is so much that I want to tell you.

Let Me take time to just be with you. It is always good. It is always so nice to be near you. Don't hide from Me what is happening within you because I already know. When you are open and talk with Me about it, I can do something to help you when you ask. Until you submit the thoughts from your brain into My hearing, I don't have the permission to do what needs to be done. You need to surrender it to Me. Then I can mold it into what it was intended to be.

Let Me know your thoughts and allow you to acknowledge them. As I share My thoughts and My will with you, we can work together. Do not fear. I never ask you to do what you can't do. I help you be equipped for each task. Sometimes when you don't feel ready, I need to push you along like My mother did with the wine at the wedding. However, if you really look within, you will find the answers. I am right there supporting and guiding you on the journey.

Do you think that I have too many other things to do than to listen to you? I can take it all in at one time. My thoughts are so much higher than yours. However, you can also have many thoughts at once. They come flitting in, and the speed at which they come is often so fast that you don't recognize them.

Take time to know the thoughts and intents of your heart. It will help to guide you.

I have been waiting for mankind to come to Me. There are some people who always come. Their time is a blessing. They come multiple times throughout the day. They are wonderful to rely on. Continue to look to those who are in My presence.

I want to make sure that you know and realize the importance of holiness. It is being truly forgiven of all the sin that is a part of your life. I wanted to have My people live holy lives. You are such a wayward people, going your own way rather than seeking to obey Me.

The way forward is rough, not smooth. That is because I build into it a way of pain and struggle to make you stronger. There are many reasons for this, but mostly that you emerge stronger through trials. Trials make you stronger and allow you to stretch and grow. They prepare you for the next trial that will come. That is one thing you can guarantee that you will have in this life—trials.

I desire to do a new thing. I want to see that everyone has freedom. I want to have people let go of the hurts and pain. That will happen by and by. However, I came that you would have abundant life. I expect you to reach out to others. I expect you to be in community. Will you do it? What is stopping you?

## Love from the Heart

The church must get back to My main message. I came to cut through all of man's rules to bring the essence of truth. There are too many ways of governing in the church. Whatever happened to the pure message I brought?

I cared for people. I looked on the heart. I reminded people to follow the commandments. I simplified them to be love God and love your neighbor as yourself. How much simpler can it be? If it doesn't pass those two things, it shouldn't be happening.

Love God. How many people really do love Me? Do they love Me all the time or when it is convenient? I desire to have people love Me exclusively, more than anyone or anything. People have chosen to love other things, and they become addicted to them. Then they no longer worship Me alone. They have so many other loves, and I get crowded out. Remember that in the Ten Commandments, I said that I am a jealous God and you shall have no other gods before Me. I am not truly loved when there are other lovers. I want to be the exclusive love of your life.

Love yourself. So many people do not act like they love themselves. They don't take care of their bodies, minds, and spirits. They get all out of balance with work, overdoing activities, and neglect the Sabbath rest that I made all people to need. People are doing so much comparison with others that they end up often feeling like a castoff. I made each person to be good. It hurts Me when people discard My work as defective. Each person is perfect in My eyes. When they don't accept the gifts that they have been given, I am rejected. I pray that people will accept the life that I have given and be thankful for the ways they are made. I pray they will be enhanced with love and desire to live as My children. I pray that they will see themselves as

I see them so they can truly shine. This is a key to being able to love Me and love others.

Love others as yourself. It is hard to love others when you don't love yourself. This is something that is troubling the world now. When people feel badly about themselves, they also feel badly toward others. When they hurt and feel that they are not enough, they often lash out on others. They find it easy to lash out on those they are jealous of or those who have gotten in their way.

People must stop comparing themselves to others. It is coveting. It causes them to want more than they need. It causes jealousy, greed, and evil of all kinds. People want what they can't have. If they loved themselves and loved others, they would just be grateful for what they had and happy for others and respect what they have.

When people hoard things or flaunt what they have, this causes more issues. Instead of sharing what they have as I intended, they build bigger barns and have more to flaunt or show others that they are well off.

My intent was that people take care of one another. Each person was given a gift that they were meant to share. Instead of sharing the gift, too many are like the man who buried the coin rather than investing it. When you invest the gift, it multiplies. When you ignore it, it rots.

I have given gifts that all would have abundant life. Why don't people use them? They are afraid. They don't feel good about themselves and are afraid to use what they have been given. They are afraid to fail. Yet I have prepared each person for the tasks that I have given them. I am always with them to help them through each opportunity they are given.

The world needs more love. I keep pouring it into My children. They are to use it so it can multiply. I hope that people will realize they have a task to do—spread My love to all people. Be a light in this world of darkness. Shine where you are. Let the truth be illuminated. Expose the deeds of darkness. I have no hands but yours. Use them for My glory and because of My love.

## Take Hold of Peace

Peace is a relative term. Peace occurs when there is rest in the body cells. It doesn't happen when people are upset. It happens when people are content and trusting that I, the Lord, am in control. Peace is not something that the world gives. It is from Me. It is an action within the body of being sure that I will take care of an issue. It requires faith.

In order for some people to be at peace, they have tried to slow their bodies down with chemicals such as food, alcohol, or drugs. These are all false ways to get to the body to rest. It slows them down for only a moment.

When I give peace, I allow the signals to have the light of peace within. It brings the body into peace like no other peace can be. It has to remain that way because of the way the light has moved throughout the body.

The artificial peace can't remain. The peace I give remains until the element of fear extinguishes it. That is why I said so many times for you to not fear.

Fear is rampant in our world today. This is not what I intended for man. Peace is the intent. Yet fear about finances, government changes, the future, and man's wonderings have been heightened causing instability. Keep the light of love going and the element of trusting Me, and these problems become less.

Peace involves trusting Me with all of life. It takes faith. It takes calmly placing all in My hands. Peace is then available to people.

People refuse to trust anyone today. They have turned away from Me and set themselves up as the person in charge instead of Me. That has caused much strife.

Oh, My friend, take hold of the peace that I offer you. It is abundant and free. You will never go wrong by trusting in Me. I am the One who created you and knows you better than you know yourself. Trust Me. Allow your faith in Me to grow. Let peace into your whole being. It is amazing what I can do. I love you more than you will ever know. Trust Me. Be at peace.

## Holy Spirit

God, My Father, has a plan. He gave the Holy Spirit to live within the souls of men. The Holy Spirit is there to guide and to remind people of My ways and My words. The Spirit shows what He has seen, and He also is there to remind you of what is important to you, especially things that will cost you time and money if you do not listen.

The Holy Spirit has a memory that draws upon the ages throughout all of time. He is wise because of those experiences. The ways that have been filled with peace and love are marked by His presence. His voice can share those memories in ways that help you to make a better choice, to live a better life.

The Holy Spirit is a support when you don't know the way forward. Trust that He will show you the way. Trust that He has your best interests in mind. Trust that He has seen success in the past and will lead you in the way that is filled with trust and lead you in the way that is filled with kindness.

As you begin to trust the Holy Spirit's voice, it will be easier to hear and obey. The right way for your life is known. Hear what the Holy Spirit has to say and allow it to bring peace to your heart, knowing that you have a personal guide within your heart. It is important that you trust Me.

Your heart will give you direction like no other. It will bring the important things to your life. It will even help you with details that will make a difference for you. In order to hear, you must listen to your heart and be still. Few people are still enough to hear. Be still and know that I am the God who helps you live the fullest life you can. I give My peace to those who seek Me with all of their heart. I love My children and will not steer them in a bad way but bring good and peace.

Listen to the Holy Spirit's guidance. It is what is best always.

## *Life*

Life is a mystery. Each person sees it a little differently because of how they are created, with differing gifts, talents, and yearnings. The environment in which the person is raised is also a big influence on the person's life. The patterns of life happen early and take a long time to change, but it can be accomplished with My help.

There are so many choices for life. What to eat and drink, what to wear, what to do, who to marry, who to love, what to buy, where to go, who to trust, to name a few. Choices happen all day long every day. It is amazing that there is any commonality. I gave people the ability to choose. Sometimes they choose what I would want. Sometimes they don't. Other influences are a part of their lives. It is often amazing to Me what people do.

Yes, I created people to do amazing things. I stand in wonder sometimes at the persistence of some people who keep going strong even when there are obstacles in their way. There are others who totally give up and walk away when there are difficulties. They say it's not worth it. What they were meant to do and to be lies dormant.

People don't use their full brain capability. If they did, they would be more like I created them to be, in My image. I am able to hear multiple conversations and keep them all straight. One thing at a time is about all mankind seems to process. Being in the right place at the right time makes a difference, but it amazes Me when it happens since all the external prompts pull mankind from their purpose.

I would love it if each person would listen to Me. I have the perfect way forward for each person. I know what would help, yet I am rarely asked. It takes time for people to give up their own will to accept Mine. They have their own ideas. Yet if they would just listen and heed My voice, their lives could be improved greatly. My still, small voice needs quiet to break through. The world is rarely quiet any more. People choose to have the noise around them most of the time. It is in stillness that I am most effective in getting through.

    I have come that you may have life and have it abundantly. Are you settling for less than what I can give you? Do you want to fulfill your purpose? Come to Me and I will lead you to the life I prepared for you. It is a good life with much joy. Come!

# Light

Sunshine is a help to people because it provides brightness. It helps people's mental and emotional being creating a lightness in the soul. It is a little light in pale to My brightness that you can't even contain. The brightness that I have is overwhelming to the mortal eye. It blinded Saul. It would do the same to you because it isn't meant for this world but for the next.

All of the light in the next world makes colors vibrant. It allows people to see inside souls and to know the intents of the heart. The brightness penetrates through the heart and mind. It makes people be more like the spirits. This brightness shines in ways that humans can't imagine. That is the way of the heavens.

On earth, the sunshine is gentler on the eyes. It helps to lead the days, and at night it is missing. Know that the days are to be used, and the nights are for rest.

Sunlight is always there. Some days it is hidden behind the clouds. So it is with Me. I am always there. Sometimes you can't see Me, but you can always feel the warmth of My presence. It never leaves. Even in the night, I am there. The light may be hidden, but it is never really gone.

Because I live within you and every creature, you should be able to quiet your soul to feel Me. It is not something that people think of often unless they have created the habit of seeing Me. Those who search for Me find Me. They are able to keep that constant communion in the spirit. I don't know why you seem to want to go away. However, it is the decision of man to not tap into the spiritual life. Man thinks that he can do well without having to tap into My knowledge and help. This is a false way and has led man astray throughout the ages.

Each of your cells contain light while they are working. The light is My Spirit holding you together and helping the chemicals to hold you together. The light within is Me. The light without is Me. Man has created artificial light. This light is not anything like the light that I bring. However, it does help man to be able to have enough light to keep learning and to aid the eyes in seeing things that are observed to be more real.

Come to the light. I am the light of the world. I am the light of the heavens as well. When you are there, you will know light in a new way.

## *Prayer Direction*

Prayer is communication with Me. Many people pray, but they don't pray with their hearts, just their minds. When people pray with their whole heart, I am inclined to answer. I desire to be a part of something good in the world, for I am a creative God, One who is always seeking to improve creation.

Prayer comes in many forms. It is a conversation. It is the cry of the heart and a way to express emotions. Prayer is from deep within when people acknowledge My presence and ability to help. I have so many resources. I can do things that people feel are impossible. So often they give up and forget even what they ask for. That shows Me they really didn't mean what they said.

I receive the prayers of the people, My people, and the world's cries. There are the cries of the hurting. There are the pleadings of the earth itself. I desire to have everything work together. Sometimes it is difficult to determine what is best for all the world as I work all things together for good for those who love Me and are called according to My purposes.

I desire that My will be done. I want so much to bring peace to the world, to restore it to harmony. This takes a lot of people changing their plans to meet My purposes. It takes the world working together. It takes people caring about each other. It takes the miracle that only I can work in the world.

Some people are so difficult to move forward. They are bent on their own ways. They don't seek My will in the midst of their lives. They just want to go forward on their own. If they don't want My help, I won't give it. I allow them to go on their own until they realize their need for Me and give up their selfish ways and their own will for Mine.

So many times when I hear My people pray, it is for the health of others. There is so much more that I desire to do than healing. When I was on earth, I spent much of My time healing physical bodies. However, there is more to this than just physical healing. I know that many physical illnesses are caused by sin and by carrying the past and being concerned about the future. I want to make sure that people have emotional healing and, even more, spiritual healing. I don't hear people praying in that way often.

The way that people pray can move My heart. If I know they are sincere and really trust Me for the answer, I will do all I can to see this through. There are often reasons that you know not of that I can't follow through on requests. There are spiritual forces of wickedness that weigh down on a body. There are words that have been spoken that block My power. There are spiritual forces that have holds on people. There are any number of reasons that complicate matters. Sometimes there is a lot that needs to be moved before an answer can come. I will always do all I can to work on this when people are passionate about the answer that I will give. Sometimes the best way that I can heal is to take them to their final home.

Praying is the best way that I can really hear your heart. I am always available to listen. I want to know you and have you know Me. It is a wonderful relationship that can be nurtured through prayer. It often helps you to know yourself better as you sit in My presence. It allows you to feel My love and My heart for you as we sit together. Sometimes it is good to just be quiet together. It helps to heal your heart. Don't feel like it isn't a time that is worthwhile. It is necessary to just be together.

Let Me be the One who leads the prayer. Let Me be the One who guides your thoughts. It seems like I am turning the whole prayer upside down, but you will be amazed at how well you will benefit when I lead and you follow. That is what I commanded, "Follow Me!"

Instead of doing all the talking, My hope is that you will listen. I have much to tell you and show you. I can only do that when you are still and attentive. Will you take time to listen? Will you pray with the anticipation of hearing My prayer? I so desire to move you to a place of healing and joy. Remember that I love you like you were the only one to love. I want a personal loving relationship with you and each one of My children. Come to Me. I will give you rest for your soul. I will carry your burdens and make the weight of them light. I will be here waiting for you. Come!

# Worship

Come, let us worship together. Blessed is the one who comes in the name of the Lord. Hosanna! Be at peace in your heart and lift your eyes to the Lord, the Lord of all. He is truly worthy of all praise, glory, and honor. Shout praises to Him. Bless His name!

It matters that you come to Me. I rejoice in your presence with Me. Let us sing a new song. Holy, holy, holy is the Lord! He has blessed His people and the nations who trust Him. He longs to be with You. He is Adonai!

Rejoice that you have in Me such perfect peace! It comes because you trust Me. Being in such a relationship keeps you grounded. You know that I am the One who holds you, supports you, leads you, and guides you. That should make your heart glad.

I come to you as you come to Me. We are able to have sweet communion. Our hearts touch, and our minds are filled with sweetness of fellowship. It makes us glad within.

Come, sit with Me a while. Let Me look into your eyes and allow you to be healed of the difficulties you are experiencing. Let Me hold you close and cradle you in My arms. We have such love between us. Take in My love and I will take in yours.

My love is meant to share with others so as you have been filled, share freely with others. There is always more as you return to Me. I am a filling station. As you come to Me, I am able to fill you with love within so that it just keeps multiplying. It is given freely without cost or expectation. The more it is shared, the happier I become. I love to see My children bringing others to Me.

You worship Me by spending time in My presence. This is not a time to complain but a time to praise and rejoice. You will know Me more in fullness as we spend time together. It is a time to be silent and listen. It is a time to be thankful, grateful for your life and My provisions for you. I provide all you need. There are many things you can do without, but you will never be satisfied until you come to Me to fill your needs.

I love you. I desire for you to love Me too, but I will never push you into that. I believe in genuine love. It is always My hope that you will choose to love Me, your Maker. I desire relationship and love. However, I have given you a choice. Which one will you make?

## The Gift

You have come to this time seeking My words. I tell you that there are times to just be silent. That is what happened to Me before My accusers after I was betrayed. I just had no words. I felt there was nothing I could say that would make a difference. Why should I even speak? I knew that My Father had chosen to make Me a sacrifice for the sins of the world. I knew it would be painful, but it was much worse than I imagined. I felt abandoned and defeated. I hurt more than I had ever known. It was a painful death. I know that My Father God could see no other way. He knew that mankind was doomed if I didn't become the sacrifice. He had a plan for Me for life. He gives life. He takes it away. I was the atoning sacrifice. It was a gift of love to all mankind.

I wish that mankind would recognize that they are free from sin. They no longer have to make that choice. I came to free them from this awful way of life, yet some people still choose to live in that way. What a bad choice! Don't they realize they could turn from sin and I could free them? I have already paid the price. They just have to accept it.

Acceptance of a gift is sometimes not available to people. They don't see the sense in the gift. They don't realize its worth. They don't know what to do with it. It doesn't make sense to them. I understand, but I wish they would accept the gift. That is why I came. I came that they may be free from sin and evil. My heart breaks that I went through that excruciating pain, and they are still choosing the torment.

Oh, My people! I so desire for you to be free! I beg of you to come to Me and lay down your burdens. Let your sins be absolved. Let My sacrifice make a difference in your lives. It came at a great cost to your Maker. If it goes uncollected and unused, I did it for nothing. It was My aim to save mankind. Will you let Me save you?

## Warriors of Love

The United States will be destroyed within. There are people already rising up to start a revolution. It will devastate many cities. There will be much hurt. If the church remains silent, it will be much worse. Church, arise! Use your voices! Let love win!

I come to help you. What you choose to do will determine the extent of the devastation. The people of God can help prevent much of what happens by talking with people and drawing them to Me. Extending love will help. However, there will be devastation. Will you pray? Will you speak up? Will you speak the words that I share?

I have put within each person the ability to hear Me. Many don't take time to listen. It is imperative that you take time to listen and that you follow through with what I say. I can make a difference in this battle, but I need people to trust Me. Will you trust Me? Will you stand for Me?

It takes people who are ready to stand with Me to make a difference. I can do it Myself, but that doesn't change hearts. What I need is people who are able to speak words that can make a difference. They won't take time to listen to Me. If you speak, they may hear, but it will have to be done more with actions of love than with words. It will take time to build bridges and to change hearts.

It doesn't help that the United States has been split along political lines. It doesn't help that people don't consider each other as equals. I created all men in My image. That means that each person has a soul. Each person has light and love within them. Some people choose to use it. Others are stingy with it. Still others refuse to acknowledge Me or My gift to them at all. It is sad to Me, but it is true. I have given man free choice. Many have chosen to go against the One who loves them more than anyone.

In order to go forward, you will need to be still regularly and listen to My voice. I can and will direct you. There may be things you are asked to do that don't make sense, but believe Me when I say, I am the Way. I know what will make an impact and what won't. Sometimes, like with Moses and Pharaoh, I use multiple things before people finally get the gist. You need to be willing to stick it out until it is effective.

I need an army of warriors who are willing to stand for love. I need people who are willing to speak the truth in love. I need people who are ready to go where I send them. I need people who are going to be dedicated to serving Me no matter what the cost. Will you join the battle? I need you.

Don't be afraid. Remember that I go before you. I know what I am doing. I know the way that will work. Listen. Follow. Obey My charge. You will see that I care deeply about people and want the best for each person. Let My sovereign will take control of your heart and life. Together we can make a difference.

# Church, Arise

I am overwhelmed by the people who are doing all they can to destroy. I need the church to rise up and stop being in their seats, passively letting this movement take control. I don't see people doing anything to stop it. Perhaps it is fear that they will die. They need to remember that death is another step in life. I want to work through My people, yet they don't seem to be listening. They turn a blind eye. They freeze in fear. They run the other way. I need the church to rise up and fight against it with love. They are not out talking with the people and caring for their needs. These people are hurting. That is why they are so upset. Hurt people hurt people. Yes, that is true. I need those who have been healed to take a step of faith and reach out to them. I know that there are safe ways to do it with one-on-one talks, but they have to be peaceful.

I didn't come to destroy things except to overturn the tables in the temple because it was wrong. I didn't lash out physically, but I told the truth. I expect My children to speak the truth in love. Instead they are just being silent. I need them to wake up and take up the cross. I need them to follow Me. I need them to be love. I need them to live love. I need them to speak truth. I need them not to sit idly by and see the world destroyed.

So many people are just doing whatever they can to pull people down. They are evil! Satan has control of them. Yet I know that love can melt the hatred and that truth will overturn the lies. It is important that the truth be told. It is important that the lies be exposed. It is imperative that My people rise up and do what is right. They have been silent too long.

I know that you feel that you need to be safe and to listen to what others say. However, you are My child. I need to come first. I am your Savior. I come to divide families. I want you to be standing in this time. I need you to speak. Please listen and follow My voice. Remember that there are other voices that will try to take you away from Me. I will always speak the truth. Others may try to take you down a different path, so be clear about what you hear. You will open your mouth to speak and not know what is even coming out. My words are true and must be spoken. Don't try to push them down when you hear "Thus sayeth the Lord."

I desire to have My people in the forefront of the world. There are many children all over. If they would unite, there would be a great army that would overwhelm the evil. Just as the soldiers went to join David and offer their services, I need My people to come to Me and offer their hearts and lives. I desire to have a great army of love uniting across the lands. People together can make a wall. They can stretch across the land as a barrier for peace, for justice, for righteousness, and for love. We do not need to have an army for protesters, just of peacemakers. Join together in love and in prayer.

If My people who are called by My name will humble themselves and pray, I will forgive their sin and heal their land. I meant it then. I mean it now. I beg of My children to receive Me and to be praying as never before.

I know that you want to do what is right. Keep listening. Know when it is time to join that it will be right. Do it. Join the march of faith. Let love win! It is time! Women, children, men, families—join together. Arise! Let love win!

## Wave of the Spirit

Rain comes so it will continue to grow more of the things I created. Winter rains help with spring growth. Snow is good, but it takes a lot of snow to equal the rain. That is why I make sure that sometimes there is rain.

Somewhere on earth, the rain is falling. I don't always choose the same place. Sometimes there are droughts. It is a reminder of being spiritually dry, not giving in to time with Me. So many people are not taking time to nurture their relationship with Me.

Thankfully, some of My children are faithful. They receive the rain well. They soak it up and allow it to be given out freely. Then they are free to soak in some more. So many times, people just want a sprinkling. When a flood of My Spirit comes, they don't know what to do. They end up wasting it.

A wave of My Spirit is coming. May you catch it and spread it. May others come along with it. May this fresh wave cause revival in hearts and minds of many. It is not meant to be kept within. It is meant to spill to the world. The churches may be filled again. The people will hear the voice of God and desire to hear more. The thirst for the Word of the Lord will be great. The purpose of this wave is not only to spread it to others but to move people into action.

People have been just sitting with the issues that are bubbling out there. It is time to take a stand. When people are willing to follow My lead, there will be positive change. Love must be the impetus for the changes that happen. Love conquers evil, hatred, resentment, bitterness, and strife. Love never ends.

In order to do things out of love, people need to drop their prejudice and hurts. To become peacemakers, it takes direction from

Me. People cannot do this work on their own. It is crucial that I take the lead. Listen to My ways and follow.

I am the way, the truth, and the life. As people give Me the lead, I will help there to be peace on all sides. Consider what I can do with all of My children's support. I could do things alone, but I choose to work through My children. I have been faithful to help them. Now they must be faithful to follow Me. It is a reciprocal relationship. Trust is required on both sides. I have trust in My sons and daughters. In order for this to work, they also must trust Me unequivocally. They need to drop all doubt and truly trust in what I can do.

My children have heard of the miracles that were done through people in the Old Testament and the New Testament. It seems odd that they don't trust that miracles will happen again. I need people to believe Me and the words that I say.

Be ready for the Spirit to move! It is ready to get started. The wave is already forming. It will rise up greater as people are ready to trust Me. Be ready!

## God's Love

The love of God is greater than any power on earth.
It is precious. It has great worth.
It fills the hearts of those who care
And blesses others everywhere.
Come to the Father, you who yearn
And from His precious Spirit learn
Of things that only God can know
And let His will be done below.
His love is great!
Oh, do not wait!
Come fill your heart
And let it start
An outpouring of fresh love that washes over all the earth
And melts the hate and heals the hurt.
Only God can do such a work within
So let Him cleanse our hearts from sin
And bring us back to His creation
As He wants to heal this nation.

## *Love and Prayer*

You are the light of the world. You are the city on a hill. You are so precious. I have made you to shine like the sun. You are radiant! You are prepared as the bride of Christ—My bride. Your love will never end. You are glorious. You have My joy written on your face and in your heart. Allow it to shine forth brightly.

Your love is able to do more than you ever could imagine. That love comes from the depth of your spirit which is the Holy Spirit within you. Let it radiate to all the world! The world is so in need of love. Spread it wide! Spread it long! Spread it deep! Spread it high! Allow My love to permeate into all the world. You can do that as you reach out to others. You can only be far-reaching through prayer.

Prayer takes you to the depth of hearts as you reach out your love to others. Prayer can cross the miles and reach to heavens. Prayer is a language that God understands in any way it is uttered. When your heart is in it, God won't forget it.

Let love go forth to all the nations and its peoples. Let prayer cover a multitude of sin and hatred. Let prayer be the sweet-smelling aroma before the Lord that allows the gates of heaven to open and send help where it is needed. Don't let hate dominate. Send love daily. Every time you think of it, send love. Keep your mind centered on God, and there will be more prayer lifted.

You have no idea what prayer can do. You don't always see its impact. That's all right. It still reaches far and wide. It is able to go where no man can be. It can change hearts, situations, and heal in the depths of the soul. Never forget to pray.

As you consider what is needed in the world, let love be the greatest thing. Yes, people have needs, but without love, the people perish in the depths of their soul. They become wanderers, not knowing what to do. They die inside without love. They go through motions, but they don't really live fully. Love is essential to a vibrant human being.

Pray for love to penetrate hearts. Let the light of love shine through the darkness, hatred, bitterness, wrath, and malicious intent. It is so vital to life. Love can melt these things and allow life to be full. Sharing love through prayer is what I require of all My children.

I have set you in a place where you may feel comfortable. However, you need to be reminded that the whole world doesn't share that same feeling. There are needs. There are people starving. There are people without shelter. There are people who don't have enough clothing for the weather around them. Pray for these things. These people need to have their needs met. It will take people who are looking for ways to be helpful to come alongside them and provide for their needs.

There are people whose hearts are broken. They don't experience love because they have lost a dear loved one, or they have been hurt so badly. They do all they can to cover up that hurt, but they are in need of healing. They will never be the same, but I am able to lead them to a place of safety. Will you pray for them to be healed? They need a touch of love.

There are those who are really far away. They don't believe there is a way that they can get out of their situation. They don't know they can turn to Me. Will you show them the way? Will you pray for them? They are hopeless and need to find hope again. They don't believe that there is a way forward. Help them to hold on. Lead them to Me. I can help them.

There are those in prison. Some have done terrible things to others. Some have lost their way. Some have just been a victim of circumstance. Their hearts are basically pure, but they made a mistake, and they are paying for it. Some of them have evil in their hearts. They need to know that I can heal them. They need to know they can take steps to be the people I made them to be. They need Me. Will you pray that they find Me?

Take time to pray. It is powerful. It can change the world. Let all My people pray. I beg you to spend this precious time to lift people up. It will make a difference one person at a time.

## Doing God's Will

The days appear long, but they really are not. The time that you live is but a moment in the scheme of time. The infinite time is what I see. It isn't for you to see and experience on earth.

Be vigilant to do what I direct so My will is done. Your work is to do the will of the One who made you. It is not to do whatever you please. It is to accomplish the work that I made you for. Each person has a place on this earth. Talents and gifts are unique so that all of My will is done. Sometimes I need people to team with others to get the work done more effectively and efficiently. Don't be afraid to join with others. Be open to what I have in mind.

For some, it is to work to share the gospel of Jesus Christ. For others, it is to listen to the hearts and thoughts of people. For some others, it is encouraging the ones who are unsure and fainthearted. I have a task for each person. When people are properly shown their gifts and use them, much is accomplished. It is My desire that the work be done so many will receive Me and be grateful.

Love covers all that I do. It should also cover all that My children do. When things are done with a loving heart, the lives of others are touched. When people do things grudgingly, there is no love or joy. Take heart and share with love. It is so much better for all involved.

Come, let us work together. You have your role mapped out. I want to make it even better, so listen to My instructions. You will see that My ways are perfect. However, you must wait for My timing for it to be that way. When you run ahead of Me, it will not go smoothly. When the time is right, all things are accomplished well. That means you must listen and wait. I know that is very hard for you, but there are often things I must put into place before the time is right. These things are often hidden from your eyes.

The way forward isn't always a straight line. Sometimes there are twists and turns like the New England roads that wind. This is because we need to overcome some obstacles along the way. However, if you pay attention to what I am doing, there will be healing and hope as you move along. I know what I am doing and where I need to take you so you are prepared properly for the work of My kingdom. Submit to My voice and heed My calls. I will not lead you astray. I am here to strengthen and encourage you with love.

Yes, it is My desire that you do My will every day of your life. Be ready. There is work to do that you know not of. I will show you the way.

# Heal the Earth

The earth and the fullness thereof are from Me. I created all things and put a part of Myself into them—intelligence. Yes, in all things. You, oh man, are not the only living thing with intelligence. I put it in every cell. I am in you and throughout all of you. Will you not honor Me?

It is for My glory that you are here. It is for the healing of all the nations that man was placed on earth. I want to communicate with each of My creation, but especially with man who I put in charge of all things. Why don't you take this charge seriously? You use resources and build things for yourselves, yet you forget to care for all other things I have made. I entrusted them to you for all time. Care for the earth!

There are times that you have created beautiful things—parks, nature preserves, gardens, even structures that are for all mankind to enjoy. What about the animals? You have caged them up and made them scarce. I made them too. Would you want to be caged? Will you not provide a good habitat for them to have a good life?

And then there are the trees. You have some forests, yes, but they are getting thinner, and it will be costly to man. Trees provide the oxygen in the air that you breathe. Without trees, there will not be a good balance in the air making it harder for mankind to breathe. Stop cutting down the forests to build more. Use what you have. Stop being so greedy and wanting bigger things. Can't you be content with a place to cook and to lay your head?

You live in the lap of luxury, but at what expense? The things I created are all being lost due to your greed. Stop! Let it be enough! This world needs healing. What are you doing to make that happen?

# Food

Look at the birds in the air. They are on the hunt for food.

Humans have made getting food so complex. They have gone from eating the fruits and vegetables I provided them to using spices and all kinds of combinations of foods. Many of these are manufactured to make it easy for mankind. They have created all kinds of jobs for people from the growers to the shippers, to the manufacturers, to the scientists, to the grocers, and all the workers in between. Then people have to make choices about what to purchase and what to make for dinner.

I made life to be much simpler. Eat the fruits and vegetables. Later I allowed some animals that I thought would be safe for eating. I know that many of the chemicals that are used today are not helpful for My people. I didn't make the body to digest them well. Those who live eating whole foods are generally more healthy. That is because the foods that are eaten contain the vitamins and nutrients that the body needs.

It wasn't until fire was discovered that I felt it was good for mankind to eat meat. The impurities from animals could then be refined and burned off. Without the fire, disease could spread from animal to man too easily. The fat made a pleasing aroma that would rise for Me to smell. That is one reason that I asked man for the animal sacrifices.

Sacrificing food for My glory was a way of showing that people trusted Me to provide them with food because they gave to Me first. I saw their need, heard their confession of sin, and made a way for them to be in communion with Me through the sacrifices. It was a way to show their sorrow and willingness to give up their wealth and their food source.

Food has always been an important commodity. All living things need food to exist. I made different food sources so that all animals and plants could exist together. The world is full of a beautiful chain of life and beauty. It all works together for the good of the whole earth and all it contains. Behold this beauty. Some living things exist to keep other living things alive. That is the mission of their lives.

Some people put too much attention on food, but that was necessary in the beginning. Mankind had to work for food. That was the work that was done after I put Adam and Eve out of the garden. Adam had to grow food to eat. It was important for keeping alive. Safety from other larger animals was also an issue, but I protected man even in the open area.

The food that was eaten at that time doesn't resemble the food that you eat today. It has grown and changed, adapted to the environment. Wheat grew well in the region. This was the staple in the diet. Trees and bushes provided fruits to eat in the wild. Eventually man learned about the seeds that could be planted in the ground to make more food.

Fish was one of the first sources of protein. Man caught it with bare hands then eventually made spears and hooks to catch them. Fish is still a good source of protein. It is easy on the digestion. Notice that I didn't use fish as people were atoning for their sins. They were generally safe at that time, but not anymore because the waters have become so polluted through man's waste products placed in the water.

Birds were also a source of protein. They are generally rather lean and could be eaten in one meal cooked in some fashion. They still provide a very versatile protein for mankind. Poultry has been used in so many dishes. This is a relatively easy food to digest. There are many types of birds used for food all around the world.

Larger animals require much more preparation in order to eat them. Man used to cut them into chunks and feed the village. It was far too much food for one family to eat. That is why they were sacrificed and shared with the Levites who could share with all the tribe. They were cooked well, and they smelled so good as smoke rose to heaven. Certain parts of the animals were more sweet-smelling than others. That is why I asked that they be laid on the altar.

Through the years, people have become more adept at putting together various foods to make tasty food. Very early, women learned to use oil and spices from the plants. They used various combinations to produce variety in the meals they served. They made pots to put over the fire. They made utensils to stir. They found sharp ways to cut things. They had a simple way for cooking but many steps to get to the desired result. It took most of the day to cook and to make clothing to keep warm. That consumed their days.

Food has always been important in the minds of people. Some people have chosen to make food their god instead of turning to Me. I do not like it when that happens. They can't seem to help themselves. They just obsess about it. It is My will that they turn to Me and give Me first place in their lives. When they concentrate on food all day, where is the time for praise and singing? I love it when they can praise and sing while preparing food. I know that people can give thanks for the food they eat. I can sustain them. However, I want to be first in their lives, not second. Keep things in proper order as I intended.

## Color

Colors bring vibrance into the world. The blue of the sky is peaceful to the eyes. The life-giving color of green is a sign of the life I have given to keep the air purified for mankind to breathe. I want there to be plenty of oxygen that is fresh and new daily. The exchange between plants and animals helps that to happen. There has been a change in the ratio that I first intended. The vibrance then has declined some on earth. Not so in heaven. They are still brilliant there.

The flowers and the birds are My most colorful choices for bringing brilliant color to earth. There are colorful fish in the waters as well. These bright colors add something new for the eye to find pleasing. The pop of color brings interest and joy to the eyes. It draws the heart to investigate what makes this color so interesting. It gives special attention to it.

Mankind uses the colors in nature to add to their clothing and material goods. It brings them interest and pleasure. In many places, people have chosen to keep the earth colors of browns, grays, blues, and greens around them. Adding that pop of color brings joy.

It is in the unusual color that people are drawn to come and see. They notice something different. They want to know more about it.

That is one reason that as I created the earth and all that is in it, I wanted to use various colors. It adds something new. It is worth checking out.

What have you noticed that you have taken time to explore? Did you realize that I made it all? Was it made by someone who used My colors to create something new? Is there something you will do to make people notice the use of color?

Colors make things come alive. Use them in every way you can to help others connect with Me. Help them to see awe and wonder. Help them to see the beauty that I created. Help them to see Me in all My glory.

## Balm of the Spirit

Peace is a gift that I give. It isn't anything that you can purchase or anything that comes on its own. My people must request it. It is an inner feeling that abides no matter what the circumstances are around you.

Peace is the absence of anxious thoughts. It gives you a sense that all is right within. It is a choice. You can take peace or choose to worry or fret. My peace is so much better than anything the world can give you. It settles your spirit and brings healing to your cells. It replenishes the mind with a gentle knowing that all is well. It may not look like it on the outside yet, but internally, it exists.

Sometimes there are things that happen that seem to grip those around you, but when you have My peace, you have an inner knowing that all will be well in the end. You begin to trust that I, God, am greater than anything around you. You know that I am working things out for My purposes. You know that all is well. It helps you to remain at peace within.

Sometimes there is an issue that tries to move you from peace to confusion. Know that I desire for My people to stay with peace. Confusion is not from Me. I would never throw you into that kind of flurry. I am steady and strong. I remain solid. My ways are so much higher than your ways. Trust Me to lead you. Be not afraid.

My peace is like a balm of the Spirit. It fills your soul and protects you from outer circumstances. Know that it is quiet strength. It can do more than anything you know. It is a gift that when accepted and used can protect you and keep you safe.

Know My peace will sustain you through all times and places. Claim it as your own. Accept the gift I give you freely. It is worth more than any amount of silver or gold. I love you. Amen.

## God's Word Is True

My Word, the Bible, is true. It doesn't fail or pass away. It is faithful and accomplishes the work it set out to do. It may take time, but it happens. I speak and things change. I speak, and things begin anew. I speak, and hearts are changed. I speak, and there is a choice. I speak and wait for people to decide to follow. I speak, and lives are changed. I speak, and there is an opening for others to do what is needed as people look for what I am doing. As they tune their hearts to hear My voice, lives are changed.

My Word is true today as it was in years past. It is written to let people know that man isn't perfect. I am. Man isn't patient. I am. Man isn't true to his word. I am. Man isn't persevering through all things. I am. Man doesn't insist on following the way of love. I do. I am always faithful and true to My word. My time is not man's time. My ways are not like man's ways.

I am trying to make life on earth better, but I need your cooperation. Too often I don't get that. My plan is to accomplish My work through you. Are you listening? Are you able to help? Do you desire to do My will and support My ways?

Sometimes you think My ways make sense. Sometimes you can't even imagine how what I am telling you can help anything. It seems so counterintuitive, yet it is often just what is needed. I have a plan. I realize the way forward takes lots of twists and turns, but it is a gift that I alone can give. When I lead, follow. Where I lead, follow.

My marvelous ways are life-giving. Allow them to support you and help you to flourish. I am the beginning and the end. I want to help with all things in the middle. You just need to listen and do what I tell you to do.

## *Life Within*

It is sad that people neglect to see the need for Me inside.
There is a lot that they don't see because they truly hide
The feelings and the thoughts that live within their heart.
I wonder if it's because they don't know where to start.
Taking time to check within is a necessary task
If people want to live a life that will truly last.
Knowing there is spirit dwelling within each and every heart
The joys that dwell within are squelched if you never start
To deal with the things that have been placed within.
Let your mind go deep and find the things that make you win.
Your life is never better than when you get to know
The gifts and graces within you and how you need to grow.
Take time to live a life that's true and join the jamboree.
Live a life that's really joyful, heartfelt, and truly free.
Be My own and just believe that you and I can be
The two that make a difference in the world that's made by Me.

## *Peace from the Heart*

In order to have peace, one must look totally to Me. I give peace that the world cannot give. I have chosen to give peace in the midst of storms. I give peace in the midst of heartache. I give peace when others say there is no peace.

My peace comes from the soul, the very heart of your being. It shines light where there is darkness. It calms the nervous system and allows blood to flow where your tension would make it slow. My peace is speaking louder than the thoughts that run through your brain. It talks to those thoughts and tells them to be still. My peace takes on a role of communication in your cells, calming and bringing peace throughout the body. It is a natural anecdote for racing thoughts that go through your unconscious mind.

Peace is from My Father. It is something that is within your makeup because you are made in the image of God. This light was placed within each human being. It is ignited when the Father is asked for it. It can remain at all times, or people's conscious mind can shut it off until they choose to ask for it to be alive in them again. God is not one to require it to be in place. This is the choice of man.

Peace is used in many different ways in today's society. However, peace is a chemical reaction within the body that brings about an alignment of cells with God. It is drawing upon the light within.

People have allowed this peace to be a strength to them and to draw their hearts close to the Father. They sense that this feeling comes from Him and that they are connected to something greater than themselves as their bodies receive this peace.

Peace flows like a river within you because it lights from one cell to the next and keeps flowing through the body as long as it is given permission. Joy works in much the same way.

As I said, "My peace I leave with you." I have known peace from the beginning, and even at the cross, I could count on peace to rule My heart. I was doing the Father's will. I know it was necessary. I asked Him to take this from Me, but there was no other way to atone for the sins of mankind.

I love it when My children look for peace. However, some of them don't know how to access it. It is through prayer. It comes in quiet. It comes in stillness. Many people don't want to go there because they are afraid of the quiet and of stopping their lives long enough to be still even for a moment.

As I have said many times, "Be not afraid." Fear will drive away peace because it makes a totally different action happen within the body. Fear drives out peace in much the same way that peace can flood the body. It sends a different signal that flows to all the cells.

In order to counteract fear, you must use your conscious mind to overcome your unconscious mind. It is a conscious effort to connect with God and trust Him.

# Giftings

You come into each new day with a clean slate. Keep the day centered on Me. I can bring you through with peace and joy in the journey. Will you take time to lay all your burdens on My shoulders? I am big enough to carry them all, freeing you to walk with Me and keep your thoughts on Me.

I really do want to keep you free. Sometimes there are things that get a hold on you. It is not the intent that it should take over your life. When there is an issue, the intent is that you will allow Me to bear the burden so you can do what is needed in the world.

Each person has a talent or a gift which I have given to help the whole community. If you still haven't discovered yours, take time to think about what brings you pleasure when you are doing it or when the product is finished. Think about the small things that bring you pleasure as well as the bigger things that seem to come quite easily.

You will know that there is a gifting when things come easily and you can see that joy is a part of your emotions while you are doing the task. Remember to give many different things a try. You never know if you are good at something if you don't get involved with it. There are so many gifts and talents that remain dormant because people are afraid to give new things a try.

There are many needs in every church and every community. I send people to certain places because they need what you can provide. It is sad to Me that people get stuck and don't want to make changes. When I encourage you to move, it is not only for your good but for the good of the entire community. Therefore, take heart, listen, and move forward.

I have enabled you to do the work of My kingdom here on earth. Will you take time to be love to others? Will you take time to listen to others so you know how to best serve their needs? Will you make time to be available for support of others?

Have you found your place in the giftings of life? If you have, use them. If not, seek My face. I will show you what your purpose is. It is important that each gift be used. Without it, people will remain hurting and skeptical of Me. When you share in the name of Jesus, it is a blessing for so many people. My children are fed with the power of love, and the whole community rejoices. Keep using your gifts. Serve others in My name. Glorify Me with your giftings. I am the Lord who heals you.

## Love the Earth

I created love in others because I am love. Love is what binds all things together. It is the epitome of all life. It stretches to the ends of the universe. It allows relationships and interconnectedness that no one understands like I do. It is bigger than life itself.

I have love like no other. It stretches far and wide. It takes up all of My heart, and it is breathed into all of the universe. It can overcome hate. It can make friends out of enemies. It can bring understanding that no one can defend or destroy. It is stronger than anything I have made. I placed it in every living thing. Watch the animals of all sizes and shapes. They all have a center for caring and take care of each other. There are families even in the smallest of creatures. The plants even have a way of loving by giving of themselves for food and shelter. They give off little shoots of themselves to start another plant. They keep the cycle of love growing. They realize the interconnectedness of all of life.

I made mankind to take care of the earth, to let the love multiply. Unfortunately, there have been some people who prefer destruction rather than love. They use the earth in ways that were not intended. They destroy what was given and make the world into something different than was intended. Man no longer lives simply. He desires much more. The light of love is sometimes destroyed in the process of progress.

Man has taken much more than he has given back. He forgets to replenish the earth with good seed. He destroys the things that I put in place instead of creating more of them. He has stripped away what was planned. He has forgotten what was important in My creation.

When love is taken away in the way of plants and animals, there is less balance in creation. These things were put there so there would be a perfect circle of love and life. Man is going to have to work hard to care for the earth so there is harmony again.

Let your light shine out love and peace. I have created these things for your good and the good of all of My children. Let them stand and not be destroyed. I have spoken!

## God's Intention for Life

In the beginning, I had a thought that the world would be beautiful. It was. It was perfect. As I created man, it was very good. I made man in My image, able to think, reason, feel, create, and love. The problem came when there were also feelings of jealousy and anger, lack of trust, doubt, etc. There became a rivalry between people to be the top person. The land became something that people took as their own. I hadn't intended that. I gave the whole world for people to dwell in. They decided to be particular and want their own space. I never understood that. When they could have it all, why would they choose to have just something that they could have and claim as their own? It was so limiting. I gave them everything, and they just wanted a little piece. People became so possessive. Where did that come from? It is a mix-up in their minds. It must have given them a sense of purpose and self-worth to have something of their own. That is not how I intended for life to be.

People were sheltered from the storm by trees and caves. They had what they needed. They were free to roam. There was food in abundance where I placed them. They wanted what they couldn't have, so I chased them away from the place that I had put them. They became wanderers. They multiplied. They were not content. I tried to take care of them, but they really chose to go out on their own.

Oh, that people would look to Me as the source of their life. I made them for this. Yet they want to set themselves up as God rather than Me. I could guide and help them if they would just trust Me. Yet they don't. They go forward trying to make life work on their own terms. Don't they realize that I know the way that would be best for them?

People complained and became so selfish. I really don't understand how this could happen, but it did. All through the years I have heard complaints. Complaints about other people, about food, about the weather, about Me, about others, and about just about everything there is under the sun. What bothers Me most is that people don't seem to want to bring those issues to Me. They just want to wallow in their angst. If they would bring them to Me, I could help them heal. That is what I do best. Yet they would have none of it.

They occasionally looked to Me. There were people who invited Me into their hearts and lives. They didn't do it consistently, but they saw a glimpse of My power and might that made a difference in their wars with others as I fought for them. What few people realized was My love. Abraham and David had a heart for Me. Elijah and Elisha had a heart for Me. Isaiah humbled himself and listened to Me. All of these people were willing to open their hearts, and I provided for them. Their lives weren't perfect. They all had issues and didn't always feel like I was leading them like they thought I should. However, there was a bond between us, one that was beautiful. How I long to have that bond with each of My children.

As the world's population has expanded, it was My hope that all would follow Me. However, the words that I shared that people were to pass on to their children have been forgotten. People are making up their own minds about following Me. They see too much corruption in the church. They don't feel that is the way to go. Perhaps it isn't. I never really planned to build a church. I planned for people to come to Me and to express their sin so I could cleanse them from it. However, I wanted to keep things simple. Organized church has become a series of laws that are even more than in the Old Testament. I pray that people can come to Me, simply, unreservedly, and full of humility. That is what matters. It doesn't matter what church you attend. What matters is your relationship to Me. I am the way, the truth, and the life. No one comes to the Father except through Me, Jesus, the Christ. I am the Messiah. I am the Savior of the world. Come. Let Me lead you into all truth, believing in Me.

I love you. I will make a way for you that will be a pathway of peace. Come. Let Me love you now and always. In the name of the Father, and of the Son, and of the Holy Spirit. Amen.

# Care of the Earth

The world is full of things that I have made and things people have made. You can tell the difference. My creation multiplies. I made it to keep creating. Man's creations use materials from what I have made, create new things, and can't be recreated on their own.

I made renewable and nonrenewable resources. The nonrenewable things have taken years to produce in the earth. Things like rocks, oil, minerals, and the like. They were put there to help all the things I created to be able to sustain themselves. I am concerned that man is using them up, and soon they will not be able to sustain My renewable living things.

Man is killing off the seeds of plants by throwing them in the garbage so they can't grow. Man is putting pipes into the ground to help the flow of water, electricity, gas, etc. It blocks the nonrenewable resources from doing their job and uses them up. There are so many chemicals being used. These aren't good for man or animals or plants, yet they keep the bugs away and make people feel like they are getting cleaner products. This is just not true. I need these things to be natural again.

Can you go back to eating natural plants? Can you stop feeding the animals chemicals so they have a chance to clean up the earth? It is a difficult thing. I don't know why chemicals have become such a big thing. People think it cleanses, but it doesn't really help. There are natural things that are being eliminated and causing other issues. You take off some things and then need to put them back in another way. You are spending time and money on things that don't really matter. Get back to the basics again.

## Man's Direction

The way of the Lord is often much different than the ways of man. I, the Lord, have put into place many things that are automatic. You don't even realize the things that your body does without even thinking about it. The world has day and night. The seasons move through the year. The animals and plants have their ways that I set in motion. Yet I know each disruption. There are times that things don't work the way they were planned. This grieves Me. It causes disease, changes in the environment, anger, fear, collision, want, and loss.

Men's desires have gotten out of control. I have fashioned man after My own image. I want things that are good, lovely, creative. Man has taken this desire and made it demented. It has become selfish, sick, and distasteful. This is not all men. It is really just a few people. They spoil the lot. They cause others to join them in the way that causes issues.

I desire to have loveliness, wholeness, completeness, peace, rest, creativity, and kindness among all. I expected man to be able to care for the environment in which they live—tilling the ground for food, caring for the plants and animals in their own area, living in spaces that are walkable, and taking care of each other and all that is around them.

Now people are so very specialized. They feel they can only do the one thing that is their own specialty. The problem with this is that man hasn't taken time to care for the plants and animals around him anymore. Man is only concerned about himself. In order to have the world like I made it again, people have got to start thinking about the earth and caring for it completely. This was My command. It is still what I need from people.

In order to stop the diseases that are spreading so rampantly, people need to get back to the basics—taking care of each other and the world around them. I know there are specialties, but where did I direct people to stop doing the basic things that make a good society?

One thing that I don't see is much community. As people work together for common good, there is much that can be accomplished. People need Me. People need each other. People need the environment to support them. It is critical that this world get back to the basics.

Politics is killing off many of the mandates that I have made. There are so many issues that the people are disagreeing about. Let's just get back to putting Me first. If My people will humble themselves and pray, I will heal them. I will heal them! I can't be sure that is what they want right now. There is so much dissention. If they would come and confess their sin, I would heal them. Will you take that step today? I do desire this as a first step toward following Me. Please hear My plea. Come to Me in humility and confess your sin. Pray. Be healed. As there are more people healed and taking care of the land and animals, you will see that My will is done. It will be good.

## *Rest and Unity*

Oh, My precious children, how I would like to see you live together in unity. That is going to take the healing of many hearts. It will happen as people humble themselves and pray, seek My face, and turn from their selfish ways. I can make all things new. It is My desire to do that. I want My children to dwell together in unity. You were made for relationship.

As you live together, each one has a task to do. There is no one who is left out of the responsibilities. We work together so that no one person is overloaded. Each one has a unique task, although working together is paramount. People must rise together and do what is right. Each person contributes from the greatest to the least, the oldest to the youngest, the strong to the weak. As you draw together, I am there in your midst. I will accomplish My work through the community of faith.

People are drawing together in small groups to make a greater difference. Lone rangers make a tiny difference, but their scope has to be so small. When they join together with others, bigger plans are accomplished. There is so much to be done.

We can feed the whole world if we share. This idea of paying farmers not to grow crops has got to stop. We need the farmers if we are all going to have the food we need for our bodies. In each area, there are ways to grow food. The big cities are now so populated that they don't have room for much fresh produce and need to bring it in. People feel they need more technology. It is important to go back to simpler times. The technology seems to make things simpler, but it is taking our resources. It is not good to have the need for so much gasoline. People need to live closer to where they work. They need to conserve gas. Using the technology for meetings rather than going all over the countryside is a better use of energy. Yes, you need more electricity to run this, but it is better than using the gasoline. People need to be careful with the resources that I provided. If they are all used up, people will be walking again.

People need to be taking time to rest. Rest is refreshing to the body, even more helpful for the mind. Overtaxing the mind is what puts the body into sympathetic mode. It cannot stay there long. Too many people are staying in that mode for weeks or months, never shutting down the stress. This will cause them to become sick or unable to function properly. It is only through the help of the Holy Spirit that this gets turned off after there is a big issue. Take time to relax. It is worth much more than you realize. It can be in short periods or in long periods. One day a week, rest for a lengthy time. Do not look back, only seek to move forward. It is important for your future and for the continuation of mankind.

I see that mankind is worth saving. I urge each one to come to Me. You are weary and laden with so many tasks. Come! I will give you rest.

## Taking Action When Called

Let your light shine that men may see your good works and glorify Me. Today this is still necessary. It is becoming more rare that people want to do works that glorify Me. They are often self-seeking and self-serving. That is not how I set up My kingdom. I planned to have people do My will and to give the glory to Me.

I realize that I gave man a choice. That choice was shown long ago. Men often choose to do evil instead of good. However, many don't realize that the choices they make are leading them away from Me. I realize that. I still long for My children to make the choice to be like Me, to live in love and to be selfless in their actions.

Being selfless doesn't mean losing their identity. It means that they are no longer looking to their own interests but Mine. I have a broad view of the world. Your view is minuscule compared to mine. You only see what is around you. I see the whole world. I hear My people cry for mercy from every continent and island. I know their needs and desire to meet them all. When My children cry out to Me for mercy, I go into action, moving upon the hearts of My children to help. I sometimes do miracles. Most often I turn to people to help other people. I know that there are good people who understand My ways, who desire to do My will, and will make a difference through their money, their prayers, their actions. It means so much to Me to have such strong warriors on the ground. There are those who listen to My voice. They know what I ask of them isn't going to be done alone, for I am there to do the work. I only need to use their hands, feet, and heart to accomplish the work. I have many people who are ready to perform My work. I just need to have them listen so I can place them right where the action needs to be.

So often when there is a task to be done, I have to see who is listening. Many of My children are so caught up in other things that they don't even know that I am attempting to give them a message. People are so into their own lives that it is hard for them to be still and listen to My instructions. It takes time alone in quiet in order to understand the message that is meant for others.

My people are so busy. It is difficult for them to make time to communicate. They are going here and there. They are seldom able to follow through with tasks because it is just one more thing to them. It is the most important thing to Me. I pray that the people will come to realize that I need to be in relationship to them continually.

You are chosen to live according to My Word. In order to do that, you need to read it and digest it, understand it, and then live it. There are many instructions there. It isn't necessary to follow every law that is written in the Old Testament. However, it is important to live by the Ten Commandments. It is really important that people treasure the Father, Son, and Holy Spirit. It is important to love others as yourself. I realize that a few addicts don't see themselves as I see them. It is sad. However, I can replace their bad picture with My picture of joy. Then they will see that I have been here all along and desire for them to embrace who I made them to be.

The important thing to remember is that I want to use you to help others. How and when that happens is really up to Me. Your job is to listen and act when I tell you to act. Be prepared to go when I call. Drop what you are doing and go. You can be responsible and contact others who are expecting you, but there is nothing quite as critical as going and following through on My call. Just do it! For the sake of the elect, do it! For the sake of those in need, do it! For the sake of My Son and for My glory, do it for Me.

## Love Everywhere

The day is full of love
For those who reach for it.
It is given from above
And it will not remit.

Love's gift is for you.
It is abundant and free.
It is ever true
And it comes from Me.

I hope that you will find
The fullness of its grace
To help all of mankind
To love the human race.

The battles, they must end
And unity shall be
As you begin to blend
All your lives with Me.

I am the Lord of all.
I desire each of you,
So please do not fall.
Give love where it is due.

It all begins with Me
So shine your light brightly

## EMMANUEL LORD

And make Me proud to see
You live so lovingly.

That is the life I planned
For each of you to live
So give a helping hand
And learn to just forgive.

Keep your heart at peace
With Me in every thought
And you will never cease
To do things as you ought.

My love for you is great
It will never fail.
Your heart I await
For you I will travail.

Remember that I care.
My love is everywhere.

## Love and the Fruit of the Spirit

Love is so important. It is the force that holds good. I give it to you. It is readily available to all who want to follow the fruit of the Spirit which is love, joy, peace, patience, goodness, faithfulness, gentleness, and self-control.

Love makes no problems for others. It is a healing balm that soothes the soul. It wants the best for people. It holds the heart close. It shows My way in the midst of pain and trouble. Love never ends because love is of God—the first and the last, the beginning and the end.

Love is shown in tender acts of kindness, a smile, a prayer, a way I show you. It is meant to be a way that I work through the people on earth. It is always available if you search your heart. As it is given away, it multiplies. It is a unique flavor in the world that doesn't diminish when it is used. It makes miracles possible. It never gives up.

Love can heal a broken heart. The lack of love or the loss of love can break a heart for a time. Sometimes it must be broken to grow because that love isn't true.

Love can heal a grieving heart when true love is lost through death on this earth. That love isn't lost, just replaced to a new home in heaven. The longing of the love that was close leaves an emptiness that only God can fill.

Don't let love sit in your heart. It is meant to be like a flowing stream giving life to all around. Love when stagnant causes pain, longing, or emptiness. Love given away brings joy. It brings even more love to your being.

Love can bring peace as you contemplate and take in My love. Be still and know God's love.

Love can be patient. It often must wait prayerfully to help someone through difficult times of learning, circumstances that result from poor choices, or times of waiting. Waiting for love to blossom in another soul as you desire to love them also takes patience. Giving the other person grace when they are struggling also takes patient love.

Love is My goodness that flows into situations that seem to be beyond our control, things you cannot change on your own. This goodness fills you up and gives you courage to live anew following the good things I have in store.

Love is faithful. This is especially true in My love for you. As you make a commitment in marriage, faithfulness is extremely important. You need to be faithful to Me, faithful to each other so you do no harm, and faithful to be who I made you to be. In that way, you are fulfilling the My law.

Love is gentle. It doesn't scream at you but comes softly. It allows peace to come in a calm way. It soothes you within. It feels like a warm blanket of protection around you. Words shared in gentleness bring healing and calm.

Love is self-control. It is one of the hardest behaviors for most people, but it makes a difference. As love rules your life, you are able to make better decisions. You can have the willingness to do what is right for you. You can live within My power to make the choices I would have you make. You can love yourself and feel empowered to love others. You can keep in sync with the Holy Spirit.

Love knows no bounds. It is infinite. It is the best thing I ever shared with man. It is forever because I am forever. God is love. By sharing Himself, God gave us such a gift. His love has power and is easily accepted. Share His love in every way you can.

## The Gift of Peace

Peace is flowing like a river. It takes its twists and turns. It flows the path of least resistance. It overflows the banks at times. It is calm and peaceful at times. It needs to keep moving or it becomes stagnant, so peace is changing with the circumstances that come its way. It continues to float above the raging water below. It is undisturbed in times of trial. It can be a haven for those who seek it. Peace comes from Me. It is a pure gift to those whose heart is Mine.

I give peace that no man can take away. It brings calm to the body and mind. It helps one to think clearly when the circumstances are difficult. It allows rest in the night. It brings calm to others who are watching the situations. My peace is something that I leave with you to help you through each moment. Claim it and accept it for your own. If you refuse to accept it, it will float away. It is a gift. Will you use it?

So many people choose to let the gift go unopened. They will never know what this holds. They will never hold peace in their hearts because they are looking for something else. They don't know what peace can do for them. Peace is better than any amount of cash, any earthly thing, any amount of friendships, or any material thing. Peace is a gift from Me. It can't be conjured up. It can't be found in anything besides Me. Look to Me and receive this gift. It will serve you well if you open it and use it.

It is far too easy for mankind to set their mind on other things. The negative thoughts can overwhelm you. That is not My way. In the kingdom, there is peace. I brought this to earth when I came. I left it for those who would seek Me. Hold Me in your heart and receive this gift of peace.

Peace is the absence of turmoil. In this world, people are in turmoil without Me. They are easily agitated with the words that people say and the things that people do. They are into having things. You would be surprised if you could realize how little you actually need. I didn't equip you with much. I provided food. As mankind sinned, I provided clothing. When the weather patterns changed, I provided shelter. As mankind began to change from eating plants to adding animals, fire was introduced. It helped with warmth and cooking. If you would go into nature, you could survive with these basics. All else is fluff.

I don't mind My people having things that make their lives more comfortable, but what really bothers Me is that they don't want Me in their lives. I can give them so much more for their spirit and their lives than they could ever imagine.

Peace is what connects us, peace and love. It is hard to accept love when there is no peace. That is why I ask you to claim the gift of peace and love. These two things can only come from Me. They make life so much better. Will you accept My gift into your heart and life? I assure you that you won't regret it.

## New Day

I made each day new. It doesn't come with heaviness unless you bring it. It doesn't come with expectation. It comes new, fresh, and full of truth. It is your job to take the day as it comes. You make it what it becomes. It is your creation.

Just as I created the world according to My dreams, it is your task to create it for good according to your dreams. Keep in mind that I made the world and all that is in it for My pleasure. Keep in mind that I intended it for good. What will you make the day to be today? Will you mend a relationship? Will you reach out in kindness and love? Will you help another to be encouraged? Will you help the earth be a better place because you are in it? Will you make a difference today?

Some people do make My world a better place because they are here to serve Me. They listen to My instructions. They have a heart to serve Me and to do My will. They know the parameters that I have set for them. They are always reaching a bit beyond themselves and growing their abilities. They seem to desire My ways more than their own. Soon My ways and their ways are merged. They have learned to listen to My voice and to act on what I tell them in their spirits.

I long to be in communication with all of My children. I long to be able to give them good things and have them share those things with others. I delight in the sharing of My children. We are one big family on this earth. It matters not where we came from or what color we are. All of My children came from Me and will return to Me. I love each one.

Yes, there is sin and hate in the world. Yes, there is injustice. Yes, there is hatred and bitterness. This is not My will. It is the work of Satan and can only be stopped through the power of love. In order for that to happen, I need the help of My children to reach out to people so they see the light and love that I give. I need to have them gaze into the eyes of those who love Me and to begin to trust again. They have somehow had their truth twisted. They have gone into themselves and made themselves the god of the world. They don't understand that I am here to help them. It is so sad to My heart that people choose their own way. I was created to help them. They only need to acknowledge Me and to ask for help. I will do it.

For today, take the love you have and share it will those whom you come into contact. Allow My peace to rule your heart. Allow the joy of Jesus to be the joy of your heart.

## Choose Well

The night is long. When the day breaks, there is a new day. It brings with it a fresh newness that gives one a new start. The old is gone. The new has come. Each day is to be lived to the fullest. What will you do today to live?

Will you borrow from yesterday's sorrow and just exist?
Will you look to Me for hope and encouragement?
Will you let Me lead you through this day?
Will you just keep a miserable existence?
What will be your stance in this day? Peace, joy, exuberance? Laughter, love, and excitement?

I pray you will choose joy and a full life well lived.

It is worth so much to live well. It is a gift to yourself and to others. It makes a difference when you share the joy. Don't keep it inside. Let it out so that others may also enjoy it.

Take the moments and turn them to Me. I can do what you cannot. I am the God of the impossible. I can make the rugged smooth and the crooked straight. I can move the mountains and calm the seas. I am able to create and recreate all things. Let your heart be light. Take this to the next level of joy.

# *Listening*

The world is but a small thing in relation to all that I have made. The universe is vast, but it supports the earth. To you, the world is big because you are so much smaller. I see it all and still care for the whole. Because I put My Spirit in mankind, I hear each plea. I know each one intimately even through there are billions in My family. I know that I have prepared a place for each one of you. There is so much more to all I have created than what your eyes can see. When you see the place I have prepared for you, you will be amazed at all that I have made.

There are many creatures that I have created. Each one has a brain. There is understanding with the brain. However, My Spirit was placed in man. Animals and plants can communicate in their own way. There is love. There is procreation. There is a way that like animals choose to be together. Yes, I designed that to be.

People are unique because they have My Spirit within. Some people choose to accept that fact. Others don't know what that means. I want to communicate My goodness to all people. I want them to communicate with Me. I want them to be prepared to help others. What I don't often see is that they desire to listen to Me. So many people are into the "give me" mode rather than seeking My will. They want to just have things for themselves. I desire for My children to help one another. As they love Me, in turn, they are to love others. That seems to be a natural way to live. Yet so many people don't come to that conclusion.

What would happen if you listened to My voice and did what I said? What would happen if you would allow your will to be laid aside and followed My will? What would happen if people would become attuned to My voice? What would happen if the words that

I spoke continued to bring life? Could the world turn around to be loving? Could the people reach out in love to others? Could the hate be melted away?

While I was on earth, I did My best to bring about peace. People didn't want peace then, and they still don't seem to want it. Yet that is what is needed most here on earth. There are people who are constantly trying to mess up others' lives with their pain leading them. Everyone who has pain and doesn't overcome it ends up hurting others. It is the way life goes. However, those who have love can help to make a different path. Love bears all things, believes all things, hopes all things, endures all things. Love never fails.

In order for love to have its perfect way, people need to accept it and make a decision to live it. It doesn't insist on its own way, so it makes a difference for people who decide to live by it. Love is something that comes directly from God. It is placed into hearts. It can guide lives as people allow it to reign.

There is a way that people can share love that brings Me joy. I love to see people sharing the Word and listening to the Spirit's voice. Following in the way that is set before them, they reach out to others in ways that are helpful. In order for people to receive the message I gave, they need to be open and receptive. It is good for us to have fellowship together. That way I can share My plans with the people who pray. It helps people to be a blessing to others.

# *Prayer*

Prayer is the way people speak to Me. They are quiet in their hearts. They can hear Me when their hearts are open.

They often come with closed hearts and closed minds. This is when people just pour their issues out. They don't really want to listen to what I have to say. Their state of mind is such that they don't have room for answers. I have to guide them in a different way than to have a two-way prayer. They are often hurting or in a hurry or looking for something in the wrong places.

Prayer is a time when we can commune together and have relationship. When people are open to hearing My voice, they take time to listen. They center their minds on their hearts and let Me rise up. I am so grateful when people truly listen and desire to commune with Me. It is a joy and helps to know that I did create people to be very good. It restores My trust of humanity. I have put all things together to make a place that man is comforted and able to take care of the world, able to hear what I desire to have happen, and able to carry that out.

The problem is that people have chosen to go their own way. They have become so entrenched with doing they forget about being the people I made them to be—to commune with Me. People are so busy doing things on their own they don't include Me in their lives.

Prayer should be as natural as breathing. It is meant to help us communicate during all activities. It is meant to fill your minds with support and joy. It is a way that you can share what is on your mind, and I can share what is on Mine. It is a two-way conversation, just a conversation with you and Me. How I long for these times. It is amazing when we come together! Oh, how My heart desires more of this type of prayer.

What some people consider prayer, I would consider a list of complaints. Some people pray for healing of loved ones and friends. I do hear these prayers and send strength to people through them. However, it is not man's mind to meddle with My divine will for people's lives. I want to have communion with you, sweet times of sharing.

Know that prayer can change My mind. If there is something that is important to you, it is important to Me as long as it is not something against My divine will. I do delight in giving gifts of love to My children. I wish for them to be content and have the joy of knowing My love through gifts. I also enjoy getting gifts from My children as they give to others. It brings Me joy to have My children joyfully give to My work.

Prayer in agreement with another person does hold stronger power and gets My attention when they are in one accord, and it lines up with My will. People who truly want the same thing for another when it is for a higher purpose pleases Me. I find these small group prayers to have more clout, and when many of My children are seeking help in a particular manner, I will do it.

There are times when I get conflicting messages in prayer. These things may not line up with My will or My plan. People think they know what is best, but I am the One who knows ultimately what is best. I have been careful to keep in mind the better plan. Sometimes people go ahead and follow their own plan without checking it out with Me first. Often I can't help them because their choices don't line up with where I was planning to take them. It gets complicated. Sometimes I can use what they choose and work it into the plan, but other times I find they go off on their own and no longer depend on Me to help. Then they complain that I screwed up their lives. They don't realize that they did this on their own.

Oh, My children. Take time to listen to Me. Your lives will be so much better if you take this time. Learn of Me. Learn from Me. Share your thoughts and feelings with Me and you will see how they become clearer.

Taking time to pray is one of the most important things you will ever do in life. Do it! Don't stop. Be vigilant in prayer. Give thanks for all that I have given you, which is everything that matters. Keep your heart light.

## State of the World

This world is filled with so much hate and confusion.
People are playing games that lead to delusion.
The nights are long and days so short that life is an illusion
Don't go too far away from home, just stay in isolation.
That's the way it is today for people forgot to share
The things that really matter with someone anywhere.
I doubt that they are happy if they are all alone.
They can't find comfort in their heart and rarely use the phone
To talk aloud and hear a voice that could bring them to their knees.
They just carry on in a world of their own and hardly want to please.
They make demands and feel they are owed a good life every day,
But they do nothing that helps out in any way.
Their lives are empty. Their hearts are dark. They can hardly stand
    the light.
They are hungry for the love that shows them things aren't right.
Take a moment, if you will, to find comfort and bliss,
I will show you that it matters to have the life you miss.
Take time to climb back in time and remember what is real.
The days that people cared for others and didn't have to steal.
These were times that people showed the best skills they knew
To make things for others that touched their hearts so true.
Let's work together in our land to do what we must do
To bring back life that makes mankind connect with Me and you.

## End Times

The day is coming when I will sort out the faithful and those who haven't accepted Me. It will be a gruesome day for those who have rejected Me. I don't want to punish, but I can't have people in heaven who are against Me. I need those around Me who have become My family. I have given love to many generations of those who have accepted Me, but in the end, each person must decide for himself or herself.

It is My hope that all will accept Me as the Lord of their lives. I woo people, but I can't make the decision that I expect them to make. Each person is given a choice. It is My hope to bring each person to My home in heaven. I have prepared a place for each one. May they be willing to come to Me.

# Created for Relationship

The world has been in crisis for too long. The air is difficult to breathe. The waters are full of trash. The water supply is being polluted. The way that I sent these things to earth is no longer how they are now. Man has really taken these things and made it difficult for people to have a pure life. The factories and cars are causing it to be more difficult to breathe. We do need people to take a step back and evaluate whether they really need all these things. I created the world to be interconnected. It was simple. I know that there have been advances, but people have made it so complicated.

What really matters?

- Love expressing itself in kindness and caring for one another
- Your word speaking honestly and making it clear to others what you need
- Your food that nourishes and keeps your body fueled with simple foods that are provided with plants and animals
- Your shelter that keeps you free from the storms (Mankind has made this elaborate when money allows. I didn't intend for people to show power with their homes. You just need a simple place to live.)
- Clean air to breathe
- Clean water to drink
- Water to cleanse your body
- Prayer to communicate with Me
- Sunshine to help your emotions and to help the earth be warmed

It is amazing that people feel the need to have all these comforts. I know that in the last century they have had more technology with phones, faxes, computers, electricity, running water, toilets, automobiles, television, radio, and the like. These are all things that are causing people to sit too much. They are working longer hours because they can see with the lights. Their minds are filled with all kinds of news and opinions. There are so many television shows to entertain them. They are getting away from the personal touches and going for second best. They feel connected falsely. What happened to conversations? Does anyone really communicate from the heart anymore?

It is My will that people depend on each other. I want them to depend on Me even more. There are so many things that I want to share with people, but they are so busy doing the many activities that are pulling at their time that I get put into last place. I desire to have relationship with My people, and yet they have come to enjoy other things. These things have become part of their world. They trust in them more than they trust Me. I am a jealous God. I want to have My people to Myself. I want our relationship to be the most important thing in each life. Sadly, this rarely happens anymore.

Do you realize that there is only one God? I am here, and I created all that is. The heavens, the earth, the land, the waters, the plants and animals, and mankind. I did it so that I would have relationship. I made man in My own image so that our thoughts could communicate. I placed My Holy Spirit within each person who became My child. Let it rise up within you. Let My Spirit speak to you. Let it draw you away from the busy life and into My arms. I so desire time with you. I desire to guide you through your life's journey. Will you let Me? Will you take time to listen, to love, to follow?

Oh, how I long for you, My child! I desire to talk with you and just be near you. Stop wandering away. Seek Me again. You will find Me if you keep seeking. I do so want to hold you again. I want to help you in all that you do. Please come back to Me. Find your way with your heart. Let it be a joyful journey for the prize is our relationship that will transform your life into something beautiful. I promise that I will be with you. Draw near to Me with faith and courage. Keep loving and hoping. Your time won't be wasted. Come!

## Lifestyle

The world is in turmoil. It need not be. I have come to bring order from chaos just as I did at the creation of the world. I desire to have a world that is in communion with Me. I made it for that purpose. I want to have the power to do what is right. Yet there are so many who have turned to their own way. They are serving themselves instead of loving Me and their fellow man. There is a reservoir of faith still out there within My children. I want them to rise up and follow Me. Yet they feel paralyzed. They are being fed lies about the nation and the world. Instead of looking to Me, they look to people. I am the way. I am the truth. I am the life.

I placed light and life into each creature I made. There is intelligence that longs for Me, the Creator. Each being knows the truth. Many reject that truth. They have decided that they are more important. They want to make choices that give them a superior footing. I have news for them. They will not go anywhere. They will falter because their will and their actions are in the wrong place. They have caused deep hurt to others by their actions.

Come unto Me and I will give you rest. Come all you weary and brokenhearted. I will give you rest for your souls. You don't just need rest for your body and your mind. You need rest for your souls. Only I can provide that for you. Come to Me that I can pour My Spirit into your wounds and heal you.

You know that there are many ways that you can get help. However, the only help that really is forever is Mine. As you come to Me, I bring peace to the very cells in your body. I cleanse your mind and your spirit. What could be better than that? It is the best!

So many people today are going after sensationalism. They want the biggest and the best things. They want to have things that are better than others. The comparisons are causing issues. I wrote in My commandments about coveting. This generation has moved that to a new level. It isn't about wanting to take their things but about getting something even better. The technology is moving so fast. It is causing the information age to be exploding. There must be a way to reign it in. There is so much out there that is false information. I know that was true in the days of Noah, but it was by word of mouth. This is almost instantaneous. It grows so fast. There are so many specialized jobs, and so much of it is about technology or using technology. There must be some way to get back to doing manual labor.

People need to move around. Sitting in front of a computer all day is not good for the soul. It isn't good for the body either. You are using the muscles of your fingers and not much else. People need to get out there and move—walking, running, using their muscles to move things. There is just too much sitting. It is causing My people to not stand straight. This will be a problem through the generations. It must change.

Allow your spirit to lead you. Don't spend time with the news and the television. Spend the time with Me. Go out in nature. Take in the beauty of the trees and plants. Look at the snowflakes. See how creative I have been in all of My work. I have been even making the blades of grass in different shapes. You will find similarities in most things, but each thing is unique. Even the hairs on your head aren't all the same color. That only happens when people use artificial coloring. I spread out different colors for highlights. I put it together in a beautiful tapestry. My colors blend in good ways. Enjoy them! Enjoy life!

# Lament

The world should lament the difficult things that are against the Lord and against people. The people whose hearts are broken by the ills they see around them should cry out to God. Have you forgotten the ways that I taught you? Have your hearts become so hardened that you are no longer fazed by the atrocities around you?

In days of old, the lament was a part of life. When someone died, there were mourners who cried aloud. When there was sin in the camp, mourners lamented and cried out for justice to be done. The prophets lamented the sin of the nation. The people were called to lament by the prophets and by the kings as they realized the sin of many. Now the sin against others is great. Where is the lament? Can you not see the need to cry out? How can you just pass by?

Women in particular have been called to lament. Jeremiah 9:20 calls for the women to teach their daughters to wail and to teach one another how to lament because of the youth that are killed off and the fact that children no longer play in the streets or people gather in the city squares. People have gone into hiding. They are afraid of doing something that might cause an issue and get them shot.

Have women forgotten how to lament? Have the people on earth become so calloused? I don't hear the cries coming up to change this situation. I see people fighting and hear of more violence. People get behind the shootings and feel badly for a few days. However, the people affected need support for a very long time. People seem to forget so quickly and move on to their regular lives. What happened to the open mourning? What happened to people just taking time to grieve…as long as it takes?

I desire for people to turn to Me in these situations. So often they pray briefly, but their hearts are not affected like I expect. I want them to really feel the pain and sorrow of this so it doesn't get repeated. Those who are getting violent need help. Can't people see how they give the warning signs of instability? Why not lament at that point? Why not get some help? Why do people just want to move on? It is worth stopping for. It is worth the time to lament. Spend the time in tears and in prayer. Instead of feasting, this is a time of fasting. I don't see that happening either.

Come to Me, all who are weary and heavy laden, and I will give you rest. You will find rest for your souls. After you have been lamenting, I bring the changes needed when you come to Me. I will act when you are truly repentant and ready for the changes to take place. Deal with people in a way that is appropriate, and I will deal with you in a loving way. Share My love with others. Let there be healing for all through this way of lament. Amen.

## *Remember*

Remembering is a good thing. I instructed My people to remember Me and what I did for them. The Jews still celebrate these times. I wonder why the Christians have dropped these festivals? They all led to Jesus. How can you go back to the festivals?

The other thing I asked My people to remember was the commandments and to teach them to their children. This has really gone by the wayside. People are going in their own way rather than in the way that I instructed them. Even just remembering the rule of Jesus to love God and love others as yourself doesn't seem to be getting the attention that it requires.

Now as people consider Memorial Day, a day to remember all those who died to give freedom for the United States of America, there are people who are choosing to make it a regular day. It doesn't surprise Me because I have seen that people are so wrapped up in themselves that they don't listen to what others have done or what I have done to help them.

It is important that people remember the things that have happened that show My power and love. The miracles that I have done are for all time. They continue and often go unrecognized except to those who are very close to the situation. There are miracles happening every day.

Think about the things that have lifted your spirits. Even the smallest things make a difference. People need to remember the smell of a flower, the beauty of the sun on the water, the clear blue sky, the freshness of the rain, the wonders of the world, the way people work together toward a goal, the blessings of the family times, the milestones in life, etc. These may seem small, but they are worth remembering.

Remember that I am always with you. This is an important fact. So many times, when you feel alone, I am there. Remembering will help you to not be in despair. You can always talk with Me. I never leave you or forsake you. Remember this. I will help you! Seek My face. Seek My counsel. Seek My will for your life. That is what I wish for every person. Remember!

## Earth

I made the earth to sustain people. It has the warmth of the sun and the warmth within. It allows just the right amount of heat for the season. It warms the world in a fashion that is perfect. I know that as resources are removed, there is a shift in the earth's makeup. This is not necessarily bad, but it could be detrimental in the end. I made earth to last forever, but with the amount of change man has made to it, it may not happen. That is why you hear of a new heaven and a new earth. I may need to make new provisions for My people.

Giving people choice was a big risk. Some people have chosen to be like Joshua and to follow Me. Others have chosen to go their own way and not to remember Me. I love it when My children remember Me. I am touched by their love. I know that it takes people some time to realize that I am for them, not against them. They don't understand why that could be. Just trust Me. I want to lead you and to guide you because My love for you is great.

Living on earth, you have seen the beauty that I have spread all through it. It is not all the same kind of beauty. It is different. I love variety. It has been a fun time for Me to see what I could do to make each thing special. Yes, there is a code for each animal and plant so they make the same type of thing. It was My light that added special touches to make each thing unique. I didn't mass-produce anything like people do today. I have a signature of love and beauty, uniqueness for each thing I do. Each living and nonliving thing is unique and special. I created it that way. Each creation fulfills its purpose.

I know that it seems difficult to understand, but the world is a gift to you. It is to support you in all that you do. The days allow you to take rest and to be working. I don't expect you to go at life with full speed ahead. That is why there is night and day. You can't do much when it is dark. You can rest and praise Me. You can think of all your blessings. You can think about how you are going to live. You can send out love. You can be at peace.

Getting out to work is important. Work is each person's contribution to the world. You can realize that each living thing has work to do. There is a way that each one has to get food. It is important so that it can stay alive. It has to ward off enemies to stop from being destroyed. It has to reproduce so there is more of their kind. These things I put into place so the world would multiply and be fruitful. I know that some people feel it was an accident. No, it was by design. I just kept creating and creating. It all works together for good. That is why I made the things I did. Yes, there is a food chain. Yes, there is life in the wild. Yes, there are shelters. They don't need to be so extravagant. They just need to protect you from the weather and the animals who are looking for food.

## Barriers

In time there will be many more opportunities to delve into the history of mankind. It is interesting how man seems to make similar mistakes. All through time, I have seen how man really wants to rise above the pain and sorrow of the world. He wants to have a better life. However, there are things that hold him back.

The first thing that holds him back is fear. Fear is a crippling thing unless it can be coupled with faith and courage to do it anyway. People get so paralyzed in fear that they change gears entirely instead of forging ahead. It is something that one can only do one step at a time. That is why each step seems like a difficult thing. However, there is no other way forward. You have to go slow in the beginning of any new thing. Get your grounding in it, and it becomes more solid in your thinking.

Another thing that holds people back is thinking they can do something alone. I didn't create people to be alone. I made Eve as a helpmate. I created families and groups of families so people wouldn't be alone. I intended for you to do things together, to help one another. Don't think that you can do things alone. Especially don't forget to include Me in the decision-making. I am here to guide you. So many people tend to forget that. If the ideas start with Me and include Me throughout the plan, it will succeed. When there are problems that come up, I will lead you through them. It is the way that I intended. Ask Me for help. If you don't want Me to come along, I will just be waiting on the sidelines, like everyone else who could lend a hand.

The dark shadows of the what-ifs are always looming. Don't let them get the better of you. As you play out different scenes in your mind, you are going too far beyond today. Yes, you need a plan.

Come to Me for it. I will show you the way. Then you do it one day at a time. Think about your next steps as I show them to you. Sometimes I know that you will be overwhelmed if I give you too much information at once. I will only reveal what is needed at the time. When I show you the end result first, it is knowing we plan to get through it together that will make all the difference.

Sometimes there is discouragement in the middle when things don't seem to be going as they should be. That is when fortitude and perseverance are very important. You can't just give up in the middle of the task. If I want you to start over, I may suggest that when I don't see another path. However, most works take time and thought. Sometimes we don't communicate properly, and things go the wrong way. Going back to square one, you will have learned what works, have some contacts, and be able to get help through things again. What is important is that you keep going because I need My people to do the things that will make the world better.

People still have their own minds. They can choose the direction they go. I so hope that they will make the decision to live for Me, to do My will, to follow My plans for them. That is the only way that love can win. I need to have the whole world coming together in harmony and peace. I desire unity of purpose and a beautiful world where each thing I created will have needs met and perfect peace. That is what I pray will happen. Don't let things get you down. Listen to My voice and follow.

## Relationship to God and Others

In the night, I whisper. In the day, I whisper. I wait in stillness for My children to come. Their minds are filled with so many thoughts. I wonder how many times they think of Me. I know that they can rarely hear Me because they are listening to the noise of the world. It takes concentration to get back to the quiet stillness. That is what is needed if My children are going to hear My voice. I long for them to find the stillness, to tune out the noises all around, to quiet their minds and hearts, and listen to My still, small voice. Can you hear it?

I long to talk with My people. I long to be able to touch their hearts with My presence. I rarely get the chance to do this now. The world has created so many things to do. Jobs are noisy. There are noises in the air from the electronic devices and airwaves of different frequencies. Oh, that you would tune into My voice. I could help you. I long to speak to you.

Your thoughts are often about all you have to do. Sports, gyms, stores, jobs, entertainment, activities, social media, games, studies, books, and so many other things pull you away from time with Me. I want to have your attention. Can you make room for Me?

I desire to have your time and attention. I want to impart wisdom and love to you. I want you to do the work that I have chosen for you to do to make My world the beautiful place that I created it to be. I planned for people to get along and support one another. I need this to happen.

I am love. I want to fill you up with love. As you give love out to others, you will be filled up again. This is My plan and the pattern I have for living in this world. Love is freely given to you and meant to be shared. I have given all you have. If you freely give it to others, and they freely pass it on, it won't take long to go around the world.

Yes, some people are hard to love because they have been hurt. That means they are going to need supernatural love, but I can provide it. I long to give it to you to pour out on others. Yes, they need this love. Yes, they can be healed of all the hurt that has happened, but it is My work. Bring them to Me. That is your task. Bring them to Me. Help them see that I am the answer. Lead them My way. I need your help to woo them. Intercede for them. Pull them My direction. Do it in peace. Do it in love. Share the truth with them. I am the truth. Capture their imaginations. Help them see that I am the way to freedom. Bring them life. I am life! I long to see the hardened criminals come to Me. Just as the criminal on the cross next to Me, I long for all to come to Me. Bring them, I ask you with all that I am. Bring them, oh, bring them to Me.

## Sacrifice and Love

I went through agony on the cross to save people from their sins. I knew this was the only way that I could reunite with My people forever. They have turned from Me and gone in their own way. I set up animal sacrifices to atone for sins early in My relationship with man. The problem was that they didn't understand and change their ways. They went right on sinning.

I wanted to do what I could to right the situation. I tried punishment. I tried drought. I tried swallowing them into the earth. I tried different ways of getting them on the right path, but they always turned. I sent prophets to bring them back. I was sometimes successful for a time. People didn't really understand that I needed them to be holy and righteous.

A few people through the ages built a relationship with Me. They made My heart swell. I was so pleased that they desired to talk with Me. I was always pleased to have them come. I grew to love our conversations. I could trust them as they trusted Me. They weren't perfect like My Son, but they were repentant when they realized their shortcomings. I so long to have others to talk with, to share My secrets with, to share My love and have it returned.

I saw no other way but to come to the earth to show people the way. I wanted to have people come to Me. I led people to the Father. I prayed and people believed. Others came through those believers, and the mission continues today. It was an opening that changed the world. It still isn't perfect, but people are coming to Me. I do desire to support those who believe in Me and desire relationship.

Many people have put their trust in Me. They then coast along and don't spend their lives talking with Me. I feel they are just waiting for something worse to happen. I hope that I won't have to go that route again. It is My intent to show love to those who seek Me. I don't want to have to go back to punishment matters.

I want to show love. My love has been challenged through mankind. I am love. What can I say? I continue to reproduce more of what I am. People give out love, and I replenish it promptly. I know that love grows as people have the chance to do things out of love. I showed love in good measure. I especially showed love to those who needed it most—people who were looking for love in the wrong places, people who were seeking and finding false substitutes for My love. Oh, that is one reason I had to show people the way.

I was totally misunderstood by the religious leaders, by those who wanted to keep things as they were. They were so rule-oriented. They were unable to receive love. That is why I was harsh with them. I wanted to have people change their ways. They wanted Me to change My ways. That wasn't what I wanted. I wanted people to understand that I had a better way. They didn't want to change.

Realizing that the human heart is open to all kinds of thoughts and misunderstandings, I wanted to clear things up once and for all. However, the ways they followed were in direct conflict to My way of love. They were jealous of My freedom, more interested in the law than in love, and really filled with hatred for others who weren't like them.

There have always been differences because I created all people to have their own mind and heart. I love diversity. It is important for growth of the mind. Would you be one who would learn, learn of Me? I want to teach you and all of My people.

I want to reestablish My sovereignty. I want people to accept My love. I want people to accept My sacrifice to save them from their sins. It takes a humble heart to accept the forgiveness and understand My sacrifice. However, it is what is needed if we are to join forces to make a difference on this earth. Will you join Me in My work? Will you allow your life to be healed by the sacrifice of God's Son, Jesus? I am waiting. Come to Me. I will help you to understand and answer your questions. I love you and trust that you are Mine, now and forever. Amen.

# What God Has Done

Do you realize what I have done for you? I came into the world to show you the way to live and love. I have loved you with an everlasting love that will not let go. I have watched you and waited for you. I have come near, living within you so that you could have My love always.

Your body is the temple of the Holy Spirit. Why would you put it through rigors that are not healthy? I made you to have a full life, one that serves Me with all that you are and all that you have. Remember that all things came from Me to start with so there is nothing you have that didn't originate from Me. I made all things that are in the world. All the resources that people are using today were placed in the world when I created it. People may change what I created into something new, but they couldn't have done it without what I provided.

All the natural resources that were placed in the earth have been used to give you what you have today. Without the creativity and ingenuity that I placed within man because I made him in My image, none of these things would be available today. It is amazing how man has used what I have given to create new things. Some have been good. Others have been used in evil ways because of the condition of man's heart.

I have the power to cleanse the heart. You have the power to share your heart with others. You have the power to do good in this world. Will you use it? There is no way that this world will be cleansed of the evil within unless people start listening and understanding the hearts of others. It is important for you to consider what you can do to touch other's hearts. Yes, they have free will just like you. However, some have given up on love. They don't see how love can have power to change a soul. It can and it will if you use it properly. When I give the sign, please use this power that I give you. Tune in to My Holy Spirit. Listen to where I am directing you. Go. Be. Do. Allow My work to be done through you. It is a good work. It will give you the energy and satisfaction like no other. Do My will always. I love you.

## *Trust*

In order to trust, you need to have an open heart. Trusting is a difficult thing for many people, because they don't really know how to do it. Trust is built on relationships. It is built by knowing someone's character well enough to know what they would probably do in a situation. Their character is shown through time. You know their morals and values as you spend time together. Trust is built when you have seen how people react in different situations. Those who choose love, patience, kindness, and hope generally can be trusted.

Some people give trust immediately to people in authority such as teachers, doctors, policemen, etc. Sometimes that works out well. However, there are some of those who have a false self and use their position to gain trust but have bad motives. They are good at hiding their true selves in front of others, but they live a second life. That is why there is corruption and trust is broken.

Gaining trust from others is a gift. People see who they believe you are and listen to what you say. Even more, they watch what you do and how you act around other people. It is the true self that they desire to see that shines like a light in the darkness. When they see good works and caring ways, they begin to trust.

Do you trust people? Do you wait before giving a blanket trust? When is it that you put up a shield and don't trust?

There is a certain way that is often used in trusting relationships. The people who meet together share what needs to be done. As they go out on their way to accomplish those tasks, some get right to it. Others are lax in their approach. Some finish the task and even go beyond bringing more ideas and contributing to the whole project in ways that are effective. Others complain about having to do it at all. Those who go forward with a good attitude and thinking more about the whole project can generally be trusted. Those who make problems generally can't be trusted.

Trust is given by God to all of His children. Sometimes He is disappointed in the things that He sees them do. Sometimes He is pleased and says, "Well done!" Many times, it is the attitude of the heart that makes the difference to God. You can try very hard and be going in the right direction but not hit the mark. God is still pleased with your effort as long as you were giving it your best.

God trusts you. He trusts that you will do what He asks. He trusts that you will obey those in authority over you. He trusts that you will make the choices that are right for you. He trusts that you will make time to talk with Him in good times and in bad.

God will give you what you need in the right time if you will trust Him. God desires to do good things for His children. When you ask Him for something, He considers whether it is good for you. He considers how it might alter your life. He considers the heart's desire and whether it lines up with His will for you. He then proceeds with an action or not.

Trusting God for your needs is a smart way to live. God always provides what you need when you ask Him. Sometimes you come to Him with wants and desires. Those desires need to be sifted through, but needs, they go right to the top. He knows your needs. He will provide for them.

Sometimes God uses others that He trusts to help you get your needs met. He wants His children to help His other children. When the person is not paying attention or tuning in, the answer to your needs can sometimes be a bit delayed. It sometimes takes time to connect with His children because they don't always want to pay attention.

God can be trusted. Man is not as reliable, but there are those who are faithful and true. They can be trusted fully to do what God desires. They are God's chosen instruments. They help to do God's will by following His leading.

Can you be one of those trusted people, doing God's will?

## *Love Overflow*

Let love reign.
Let it penetrate within you.
Let it shine out as you share it with others.
Let love do its perfect work and heal hearts around you.
Let love keep spreading as you give and give and give.
Let perfect love overflow today and always.
Amen!

## Love in Abundance

The love that I have for others originated long ago. My heart reached out to create people. This is a heart message to My creation. I love you! I wait for you to come to Me. I feel like you will be My redeemed ones. Please take time to listen to Me. I am the Way, the Truth, and the Life. I am the Alpha and Omega—the first and the last. I enter into every heart. Some acknowledge Me. Others don't. I come to all. I rejoice when people come back. I always wait for them to acknowledge Me.

Will you acknowledge Me? Will you be one of those who claim to be My own child? I long for that to happen! I know that I have waited a long time for some, but I have patience and can wait. When people are ready, they will come. What pains Me is that I know some will never come. The pride in their heart has caused them to be blinded from the love that I placed within them.

You need to be humble in order to come to Me. When you have pride in your heart, you are not seeking Me. You are seeking to puff yourself up. I am happy with the people that have come to Me and want to sit at My feet to learn and grow and change their lives into what I intended for them. They don't realize that I have the power to set them free from the chains that bind them and keep them tied in knots. I have come that they might have life in abundance.

Abundance—that is a fullness of life that people may have when they allow Me to be the leader in their lives. I can restore all that has been taken away. I can bring peace to the heart and strength to the weary.

So many people don't know My love. They may believe in Me. However, really accepting My love is a step of faith. When you accept My love, there is a genuine peace that floods your soul. It can't be taken from you, no matter what circumstances are being sent your way.

My love is full. It is freely given and freely received. It costs you nothing. It cost Me My life. My Father gave it back to Me as a gift to the world. I am always with you because I went away and returned. It is the miracle of life that the Holy Spirit dwells within you. He will remind you all about Me. Trust that this is good. Trust that it is lasting. Trust that it never departs. I will be able to cleanse you from the inside out as you allow Me to do so. It takes an act of your will. It is My will to have you cleansed and whole. Will you allow Me to do that for you?

You can be sanctified as holy and righteous as you allow Me to cleanse you from within. Then sin will not have a hold on you. You will be free to follow Me fully. That is My desire for every person in the world. Come unto Me and I will give you life in abundance. Yes, come!

## *Blood*

For the blood is greater than the water. I came to give My life in ransom for many. The sins of the world were looming big. The confusion of all the laws was overwhelming. I came so people may have life—clear, straightforward, full-of-love life. I felt that it was needed. I could see no other way to redeem mankind, so I came.

I was tired of seeing that people come to Me only in desperation. I wanted to live with people on an everyday basis, not once in a while. I came. I chose a group of people to be My disciples. I taught them the ways that I hoped would multiply in My absence. I believe that they understood what I was showing them.

Some got it right. They began to see that they also could do things in My name. They could heal and do miracles.

What I didn't count on was the opposition. Opposition has always been there. People desire their own way rather than following Mine. They tend to trust in themselves and in what they already know. They are in fear of the unknown. They rarely take a step to do what I ask them to do because of the fear.

People didn't want to change when I was with them. In fact, they opposed it in a great fashion. They were not willing to make love the way of life. They would rather be uncomfortable and depend on their own selves than to depend on something they can't see. Oh, ye of little faith! Times haven't changed people.

Faith is so needed. I have already provided all you need. I gave My life that you might have life abundantly.

I gave My love that it might be multiplied as it is given, yet love remains dormant with so many. Love can change the world one person at a time. It is important that love be given often.

My blood was shed. As you remember Me in communion, remember that blood cleanses you even more than the water you use to cleanse your outer body and your body systems. My blood cleanses the sin that so easily entangles you because you live on this earth. Take it and drink it in deeply. Remember that I can eliminate sin, but you are to go and sin no more. In order to be totally cleansed of sin, it needs to be confessed, forgiven, and washed in My blood. Go and sin no more.

# Commands

What is it that man should do? My Word clearly spells out that man is intended to love Me, to put Me first in all things, to communicate with Me about everything. Man is not to have other gods—things that take precedence over Me. Man is to give honor to My name, not profane it. I want first place at all times.

Man is to take a rest one day each week. Rest and relaxation are required for the body, mind, and spirit. It helps to renew your life. It is a time for reflection, for family conversation, for prayer. The body needs rest to recover from the hard work it does throughout the week whether it is mental energy or physical energy that is used.

Man is to honor parents. This is important, and many have not considered they wouldn't even be here without them. They owe their very lives to their parents. They are worthy of respect and love.

Other things in My commandments are a way of honoring other people. Do not kill. Honor the vows that married couples make to each other, and don't violate people by having sex out of marriage. Don't take things that don't belong to you. Be truthful in all of your speech. Be content with what you have. Don't desire what belongs to others.

As I told you, love God, love yourself, and love others, even those who appear to be enemies. This will allow you to live in peace with God and man. It will help you to have respect for others.

I also told man to care for the earth and all that is in it. By taking care of the animals, plants, and the environment, all that I made will remain good. The earth will produce what is needed for all that I have made if it is not abused.

I gave clues throughout time of the place where I dwell. The heavens are being prepared for man to live eternally. I desire to be with you even now, so I sent the Holy Spirit to indwell your hearts. Let Him guide you always.

Can you learn to live within these guidelines? They are not too hard. They are to give you love and peace. They are really all you need for a full life. Everything else is just a comfort or convenience. Other things don't matter for eternity. These things do. Concentrate on them. Make them a part of your daily life. Know that I love you and set these parameters to give you abundant life and peace that passes all understanding.

## Glory on the Earth

The whole world is full of My glory. Glory! Look at the wonderful things I have made, their intricacies and designs. How could you even think of anything but glory? I made a truly beautiful world. It is amazing how it was all put together in a way that supported each thing I made. It truly is a glorious world!

I rejoice that I have made man in My image to care for the earth. In some respects, it is a task that is more for each thing I created. Man is the keeper and the one that I intended for My help in keeping the earth clean and going strong.

It is a very good thing that I established that each living thing would procreate on its own. Man could never take that and know what to do. I expected that man would understand how to prune trees and follow My lead in the care of what I made. Since I made man with the ability to choose, sometimes My word was not heeded. Sometimes man goes off on his own and forgets his Maker.

My intent for those that I created was that they would support one another. People and animals living in groups of families would help each other to survive and thrive. Right away the feeling of jealousy caused death. There have been ill feelings toward one another, hurts beyond what I could have dreamed, and evil that has raged. That was not My intent for the world. I hoped for harmony and unity.

In order for My glory to be seen on the earth, people need to have hearts of love. They often look for the wrong things and miss the beauty and the display of glory all around them. It is indeed a beautiful world in each and every season. Each thing that was made was done with great precision. Enjoy it!

## Stillness

Be still. Let My words sink into your soul. I have the beginning and the end. Right now, we are caught in the middle. There is a calm in the midst of the storm. Can you feel it? Let it settle into your soul.

Peace comes at a price. I have come that people may have peace. In order to have peace, they must use their minds in a way that connects with Me. I am the way to peace. By concentrating on putting Me first, it will happen. Without My love and direction, peace will not come. I already paid the price at Calvary. It was done once and for all. Did you hear that? For *all*.

It doesn't matter who you are or what you've done. I love you. That goes for all people who have been born. I planned the propagation of each species. I placed My love within each person. Some people have chosen not to accept it. I rejoice that others have chosen to accept it.

My love is so deep and so wide. It reaches to the highest heaven and the lowest ocean. It is great enough to multiply itself in the world. It is transcendent enough to pour into heaven and last forever. My love never ends.

I have come that people might have this love and peace that passes all understanding, peace that will move through the passing of life, peace that will keep you grounded through life, peace that allows chaos around you yet keeps you centered on Me. This kind of peace can only happen when your mind and heart allow Me to lead. As you trust Me to do that, I keep your heart in perfect peace because your mind concentrates on Me and what My will is for you.

It is important that you practice the stillness. It is in the stillness that I can direct you and bring you peace. Stillness is at the center of our relationship because it allows your mind to be free to let Me speak. I truly have so much to say to you. Unless you are still, you don't hear My still, small voice or My whispers. I can talk louder, but it isn't My way. I know people are listening when they are still most of the time.

Be careful to empty yourself of your own thoughts when you are coming to Me in stillness. When your mind is full, there is no room for more. Empty yourself and hear what I have to say. Clear your schedule so you can do what I want you to do. Be ready to go into action but not ahead of My call. I know the perfect timing.

Stillness leads to peace. It allows you to be filled up so you can give out to others. It gives direction and helps you to do what needs to be done, even if it is hard, because I walk with you through the situation. I will lead you one step at a time. If you don't know what to do, ask Me. I delight in leading My children who love Me. I want to make your life full of love, peace, and joy. It all starts with our communication. Keep seeking Me with all you are. My love for you is great. Hallelujah! Amen!

# Give Your Cares to God

Let your heart be light. There is no need for heaviness. You can let Me shoulder the heavy burdens of life. Bring them all to Me. I am the One who knows the way forward. It is man's pride that won't allow him to give the issues to Me. Man believes that he is capable of going forth on his own. That is not the truth. I know the way. He would be much further ahead following Me.

People get stuck in their life and in their relationships because they think they know what is best. They don't stop to think that their Creator has insight they will never have. They look for insight from other people, from books, from all kinds of sources, but they don't come to Me for the way forward very often. They could be so much further ahead if they would listen to Me and follow where I lead. Those who have made significant strides in life and truly made a difference have had at least some insight from Me. They have taken time to seek My will and My way for them. They have asked the question, "What do you want Me to do, and how do I go about it?" They have taken time to listen and seek My answers.

The love that I have for My people is great. I have enough to share with the whole world. Yet there are so few people who genuinely want to spend time with Me. They go about their business and think they are doing well. Oh, but they could do so much better and have a much more direct way if they would just listen and follow Me. I delight in those who take the time to seek My face and to know My will for them and for this world.

The secret to being successful in the eyes of the Creator is to follow Me. The Holy Spirit will guide you if you will allow Him to do so. The Holy Spirit lives within each believer. He is so close yet treated as so far away. I sent the Holy Spirit so that people would always have Me within them. Yet they don't take advantage of Me being right there. They tend to ignore or forget that I even exist. They think they can do it all on their own. I have to just give this up and let them go their own way until they realize that I am the way.

There is a longing within each soul to follow Me. There is a burning desire that I placed within people. They keep trying to fill that space with other things. It is an emptiness that only I can fill. I don't have any other way to have it happen. The soul has a place for Me to communicate with you. Until that connection is made, it is empty. People try to fill it will all kinds of things—food, drugs, alcohol, shopping, gambling, etc. It doesn't help. That is because the only thing that can fill it is Me. Until people realize this, they will be yearning for that relationship.

It is relationship with Me that makes the difference. If you would get to know Me, the emptiness would be filled. It won't undo all of the things that you have done to fill the gap. That will take time, but I can heal you. You must want to have relationship with Me more than all the other things you have done to fill that hole. Your desire and your determination to put Me first in your life will be what allows all those other things to drop off. You will change your thinking and you will be made whole. Your actions will change as you put Me first, and you will find peace for your souls.

That is why I said that your heart needs to be light. Stop carrying the weight of the world. We were meant to shoulder things together. Your concerns become My concerns. My heart can take it all. My love is great, and I desire for you to be whole. Bring it all to Me.

## Love Always and Everywhere

In the stillness, keep your head up. Notice the things around you. Be filled with gratitude for what I have given you. All good things come from Me. I know your needs, and I desire to make sure they are met. I don't go overboard unless I really want you to be amazed at what I can do. When I want you to see My glory, I lavish you with love.

I am sure of one thing: My love for you is true. I am love, and I have the ability to love all of My creation. Love is action. It is the one thing humans have that flows through all the universe, like Mine. Don't take this love for granted. It is powerful. It is from beginning to end. It is deeper than the ocean and wider than the sky—infinite! I have placed that powerful love within you. Use it for good.

My love encompasses all. Human love is not as broad. People have the choice to love. There are also other feelings within a person that sometimes get in the way of love—resentment, hatred, hurt, abuse, jealousy, and the like. I want you to make plans to overcome the issues that get in the way of sharing love in abundance. Rid them out of your life. Allow all that is good to shine.

Do not grow weary of doing good or sharing love. Remember that those who really need love don't want to receive it. They may feel unworthy or that it conflicts with other things going on in their life. Some people just don't know how to receive love. You can help them. Let your light and love shine. Help people see and know the wonders of My love.

Send love in every way possible to all you can. Love has the power to travel far. In prayer, love can go around the world. Remember to pray and send it out.

Send love in every note you write. Send love to each person you meet. Send love widely and often. It is such a needed component in this world. Remember I love you. I love each person in the whole world. Help them to know it.

## Light and Love

In the night, I am there.
I heal every care.
Surrounded by light,
I dispel the night.
My Spirit is there,
Caressing each care
So that people are free
In the light of eternity.
Let My light fill the sky.
Sing praise you and I.
It is peace to My soul
To make you all whole.
I know it is true
That I died for you.
Come, be thou My own.
I don't want to be alone.
Come stay by My side,
With Me do abide
For I am Your light.
You are My delight.
I wait for you.
For you I pursue
Until you come unto Me
And I shout with glee.
You are My own.
I cry not alone.
I come from above
That you might know love.

## COME LIVE LOVE GUIDANCE FOR LIFE

My love is so deep.
Do not go to sleep.
Spread the love wide.
Don't let it hide.
All people should know
It makes you aglow
For I am the light
Of the world.

## *Honor God*

I am the light of the world. God sent Me to the earth to bring light closer, to exemplify love, to show light to the mind and heart, internal light for eternal life. I am God made flesh. I am the image of God to the world. I am spirit and truth. God dwelt within the Me as I lived in the world.

I am the Son, who came to be the Savior of the world. Men needed a way to be rescued from sin. Sin crept into the world and corrupted mankind. There was no good way to bring them back to Me. I tried through many people, but each one had an issue. There were many who gave themselves to Me in relationship. Their hearts were often drawn away. I found that man created rules that were so stringent that they became slaves to the rules rather than relying on Me. They thought that was the way to Me, but they were caught in sin and unable to really follow Me because of the social norms of the rules that invaded all the customs of the world.

I chose a remnant of people to have relationship with—the Jews, the nation of Israel descended from Jacob. These people were to be a group that perpetuated the joy of being in communion with Me. They continued to stay and to want what the people around them had. It drew them further away from Me.

I want My people to live freely. In order to do that, they need to put Me first. Those first three commandments are musts. People really didn't understand that more than anything I desire to have relationship with them. I wanted to be honored by them. I wanted to be loved by them. I wanted them to realize that I could provide what no man could provide. I wanted to be their all in all.

The first three commandments have been broken over and over. People put so many things before Me. It can be anything—a person, food, alcohol, shopping, work, sun, nature, to name a few. Whatever takes the heart of man rather than Me is a god or an idol to them. I had no intention of anything being more important than I am in a person's life. That is why I said that no one should make an image of anything and worship it. I am the only One that should get your praise. I am spirit. I dwell with man by living within now. Those who ask to have Me come into their lives know Me. They are the ones that honor Me. Yes, they stray. I desire to keep them on a short leash and to bring them back. My love is a strong force and can draw the wayward child back to Myself.

There are now many who use My name as a curse word. It is used when bad things happen. It is used in ways that punish others. It is used for emphasis. It is used in ways that cut at the heart. If man had a hold on Me, I would be lost entirely, cut down to nothing.

Thankfully, I am spirit and truth. These things really make Me sad, but they don't change who I am or what I can do. They do limit My willingness to work in their lives because I don't have permission to reign in their hearts and lives.

I desire to be able to have all My children go to heaven. I have prepared a place for them. Some won't want to go. They have chosen not to accept this gift of eternal life. They have convinced themselves that heaven doesn't exist. They forget that I have made a way for them through Jesus to be grafted into the family.

I came for true redemption. All who believe in Me shall be saved. They shall have eternal life. They will also have a full life in the spirit as they live on earth. They need to remember that I came to guide them, and as I returned to the Father, I sent the Holy Spirit to dwell within them.

Forever I will dwell with man. Forever I will be seeking those who have lost their way. Forever I will love My people who choose to love Me and honor Me with their lives. I am the eternal spirit, the first and the last. No one comes to God except through Me. Come, dear children. Come!

## What Is Love?

Love is Mine, for I am love. I love purely. I love others with My heart from the very depth of Who I Am. Love comes naturally for Me. Love can cascade down mountains. Love can reach the depth of the ocean. Love can reach the highest heaven. Love, My love, never fails to do what I sent it to do.

Love is more than a feeling, although people often see it that way. Love is an action that allows Me to be seen more clearly. It brings life and hope and healing to the world. Love covers a multitude of sin and wrong. However, it is often misunderstood.

Love is a pure feeling that can touch hearts and cause there to be more kindness, caring, and joy. Love can bind hearts together. Love of husband and wife is a love that isn't easily broken when they keep Me at the center of their relationship. I enjoy helping others to be loved.

Love is more than a feeling. It is an action that takes root in the heart. Because you love someone, you want to show them in kind ways. You want to do things that surprise them and please them. It shows the depth of love inside.

Your love can grow greater. It can give great strength. A love for husband and wife should grow deep. It is a support that cares for the other as much as or more than for self. It bubbles up and creates joy within your heart.

Love is patient. It doesn't rush others or have them have to rush their decisions. It allows the people to contemplate what is right. It leads them to good decisions because they are doing it from a heart that includes Me. They are able to go forward knowing My will and their own will have united.

Love is kind. It is able to give without needing to receive in return. It reaches out because there is love in the heart of the giver who wants to do something nice for the person who they love.

I have told you to love your enemies and to pray for those who persecute you. Love is an act of grace, giving unmerited favor. Love can cover over a multitude of sin. It leads to forgiveness and to showing mercy, giving not what is expected but what can be an unexpected gift. This kind of love can only come from Me because mankind is not capable to giving love in return for hatred. Ask for My love for others and I will give it to You. This is the way that our world can turn around. This kind of love is the pillar of faith. It is what I can do that mankind cannot do alone.

Love isn't arrogant or rude. Remember that you can get more accomplished with honey than with vinegar. Give people the best of you with My help. Guard against the lashing out and cursing. Learn to love others and honor and respect them as My children. These are your own brothers and sisters. They are on an equal playing field with you. Don't put them down. Lift them up. All people deserve to be treated with honor. Do it well. Take it even beyond what you think. Don't lift yourself over others. Don't make comparisons. It is awesome when you realize that all people are created equally. They are all My children. Treat them well.

Love doesn't insist on its own way. This is a key because mankind is selfish without Me. Love within allows you to give up your will to accept My will for you. It also allows you to give up your way to help another. Remember that you need to be flexible, pliable in My hands. I will shape you into what is needed for the time.

Love bears all things. I know there are some things that you prefer didn't happen, but you don't know what I am doing in the midst of these circumstances. Sometimes they are there to help you grow. Sometimes they are there because of the evil in the world, and it just happens. I will be with you, for I am love. I will shoulder the burden if you give it to Me. I can take it. I can lead you through each burden.

Love believes all things. It believes the best for others. It believes that I am the Lord of all. It believes that I can do all things, that I am sovereign, and that I will do what is best for My children. There are times that I need to take them to their eternal home. There are times that I will heal them. There are times that I will let nature take its course. Don't feel that I am going to magically change the world into a utopia. There are things that I can do. Good things take time. Believe that I will do what is right and good, best in the situation.

Love hopes all things. Hope gives one courage to go forward. Love plans to go forward. It is something that will not die. It helps people to hang on when there is little that shows a promise ahead. Love keeps the fire of hope burning. This love that burns in your hearts is from Me. Let it burn brightly.

Love endures all things. Love can help you through each situation. I love through all time and eternity. My ways will not end, and My love will endure through each situation and through all of time. I am love, unchangeable, and enduring forever. Because I endure, I can get you through all things.

Love is the greatest. Love is Mine. Love is the part of Me placed in every human being. Love is the greatest and strongest emotion in man. Let it rule your heart and life. It is good. Amen!

## The Light Shines Within

Light is the absence of darkness. Light is given new every morning. Light dissipates the darkness. It is better to shine a light when you walk. Remember I am the light of the world. I shine in the darkness of the soul and help you know the sin that has seeped within. Only I can penetrate the soul and remove the darkness.

Dark thoughts are becoming more prevalent as people walk out on their own. Many have forgotten that I am the light. They are tormented by fear. They are unable to understand where they need to go because they no longer look for the light.

This world is going to need light. I am always available, but so many aren't remembering to seek Me. I may be found. I will be with any who call on My name. If only they would come to Me. The burdens are great. People are weary from working so many hours on their own, from trying to solve their own problems, from going through life alone. People need Me. They need each other.

As people have isolated, they have become less willing to reach out. They have become afraid of others even within their own family. They need to reach out and see love again. They need to be led to the light.

One who is in darkness can't bring light to another. One must be connected to the light to be able to share it. I need My people to rise up and begin sharing the light. It is so important that people help others to see what I am bringing to them.

At first, people might see the filth of their lives when the light shines in. It might be too much for them to bear. That is where the lament comes in. Lament is a time of sorrow for what has been that is not good. People may realize their ways are not good. They may see that they have become selfish or disconnected or have anger and resentment for all that has happened around them and within them. They may not want to look at it. My hope is that they will turn to Me so I can heal them. Many will not know where to turn. They might seek to talk with someone, or they might just continue to go it alone. People will make much better progress if they share with someone else who has the light and have already worked through this issue.

It is good to have others who know a similar story and have been healed. It helps those in darkness to know there is hope for light to make a difference for them. One step at a time is all that is required. It takes time to make progress, but with the help of a person who has been through a similar issue, there is comfort and hope.

Light exposes the darkness and dissipates it. People need to see the things that are dark and holding them back from the light. As they see it, they may become sad. They may want to hold onto it because they don't know what will happen if they let it go. People are strange that way. They hold onto pain and agony because it is familiar. Oh, that they would let it go! Then I could lead them to new life in the Spirit.

There is so much that I could do if I am given a chance. I can set people free of the bondages, the pain, the suffering, the sin, the anguish. How I long to be able to show them what I can do. As I shine the light on their souls, on their lives, on their baggage, I can change it all. The issue is that I let man have his own will. While My will is to heal, man gets a choice. Oh, that he would choose life! I would give it in abundance. I have the rivers of living water that can flow and keep man fresh and clean day after day. This is My desire. Will you allow it?

As you are healed, you are to let My light in you shine forth. It will dissipate the darkness too. When I can't reach someone, I send My people to do the work. All you have to do is shine the light and lead them to Me. I will finish the work.

I am yours, and you are Mine forever and ever. Amen!

## Darkness to Light

It is night. There is darkness all around. I don't see the darkness, for darkness and light are the same to Me. However, it is a dark time in the world right now. There are people who are not following My ways. They are in life for themselves. They rarely think about how their behavior affects others and the whole world. Everything works together. In My world, things work together for good. It is becoming harder for Me to do this work on earth. It has become dark because they are not following Me, the Light of the world.

Oh, My people! I created you to follow Me, to do My will here on earth. You have chosen to do your own thing. You have become self-serving, going about your own way. You no longer listen to My still, small voice. If you would, I know you would turn and follow Me. I created you to do that, but you have chosen another path that is leading to destruction.

I designed you with light in every part of your being. Don't let the light go out. You need to let it shine. You need to nurture that light by coming to Me so it will be bright again. Pay attention to the inner parts. That is where you shine. It isn't so much what you look like on the outside, that outer shell, but what happens within you.

You have a marvelous light within you. It is called the Holy Spirit. Get in touch with Him. He is your personal guide to show you all that is true about Me, Jesus, God in the flesh. The Holy Spirit will point you in the right direction if you will listen to Him. His job is to point you to Me. He is ready to do His job. Are you ready to let Him?

Bring your heart to Me. Let your life be changed. Give up the old self which is corrupted. Live in the newness of life which is full of love, hope, joy, and strength. I desire to be in touch with you. Can you take time to let Me speak to you? Can you make time to get in touch with the Holy Spirit within you? Don't say it doesn't matter. It does! It is what will save you. As you share it and people continue to share it, the world can be renewed by the power of the Holy Spirit who lives within you. Let each one reach one. It will transcend human understanding. God's ways are so different from man's ways. As you take that step of faith and share it with others, you will be amazed at what I can do to transform the darkness into light again.

This is not something I want to do alone. I want the cooperation of all of My children to do this work in the world. This is a full-out effort of every person. It starts with one. Will that one be you?

I pray that you will be filled with courage and confidence, knowing the truth of the Holy Spirit. Share that truth with confidence and joy. When people see that you are not afraid, that fear has been conquered and joy abounds, they will inquire of you about the change. Be bold! Share your story. Allow it to change others. Keep telling your story. You never know how it will affect others. I will prepare hearts. It isn't your job to determine where the fruit will come from. Just share your story. Share it in love with great joy. I will work on the harvest of souls. That is an inner work. I will see to it that there will be some who will hear and follow. You are not responsible for others. You are just to do your part and share.

When people start to see the light, continue to pray. Help them to know Me. Lead them to My Word. Help them to pray. So many people don't want to pray because they are afraid. Help them. Pray with them. Pray for them. Pray for My will to be done in them.

Allow My peace to lead you. Yes, you may feel uncomfortable at first, but as I give you holy boldness, you will be My messenger of truth. Don't stop! Keep sharing what I have done for you. It is necessary to bring others into the light.

My way is full of light. I continue to shine always. Look for the light. I am shining even in the darkness. It only takes a little light to lead the way. Reflect that light to others. Soon the world will be bright again.

## Dwell in the Light and Truth

It is the dead of night. People are living in darkness. They barely see the light. They are going around groping for truth. They listen to the lies of the evil one, and of so many people who are living in fear die to the voice of the evil one taking over their thoughts.

Those who dwell in the light of My healing presence will live in truth. They will see that love guides their days. They will be free from the enemy as long as they cling to Me. They can lead the others away from the darkness. But they need to listen to My ways in order to do it. I will lead them in truth. I will show them how to do it.

I am the way, the truth, and the life. No one, I repeat, no one comes to the Father but by Me. I am the one who leads people to the light, to the source of all truth. Do what can be done. Listen to Me.

In order to live in the light, one needs to be able to see. I blind those who are not of Me so they don't know what they are doing. Those who are filled with light have the ability to do all things that are within My will. I show them what it is that I want done.

You are My child. You can dwell with Me in truth. You have knowledge that others know not of. I whisper in your heart, and you hear Me. Can you listen more often? I know there is so much more we could accomplish together if you could take time to hear. Then you would know how to follow.

I want you to help those in darkness. Help them to be enlightened. Let them know there is a way out. They just need to know that I am their source of all good. Talk with them about Me. Help them to be surrounded with people of light. Help them to see that they need Me. Share with them all that I have done for you. Tell your story. That's all it takes. One person sharing the story can plant a seed that grows. Sometimes it takes several people sharing their stories to make a difference. Tell the stories. Let people know that I am still alive and living within the people. I placed My likeness within each one. The enemy has stolen thoughts and swayed people with his lies and deception. People have loved the darkness and ignored the light. They don't realize the cost of the darkness and how it captures them and hampers their lives. It usually happens so subtly that they don't realize it until it has gone so far that they are in great darkness.

Live in the light. Shine it brightly. Don't wait for others to do it. You be My witness. That is what I need. Shine! Share! Be a conduit of light! I need to flow through people. Being stagnant and pushed down, I feel squashed. Rekindle the fire that I placed within you. Shine brightly! Keep My light blazing within you! Speak with Me all through the day and night! That way darkness will be overtaken by the light within.

I love My people. I am so sad when I see they are overtaken by darkness. Help them see the light. Build up their hope. Show them My love. Minister to them in kindness and gentleness. They will come and join you as they are rekindled with the light. Shine for Me. Let Me shine through you. Be My faithful witness to the world.

## Our Example

Listen, My children.
I am good.
I created you to be good.
Lean on My Spirit.
Let Me direct you.

I want your love.
I want your heart.
I want your obedience.
I want your help.

I have come to heal.
I have come to love.
I have come to give life.
I have come to anoint.
I have come to lead.

Will you follow?
Will you love Me?
Will you love others?
Will you take My hand?
Will you do what I say?
Will you do what I do?

I live so you can live.
I love so you can love.
I give so you can give.
I died so you can live.

EMMANUEL LORD

When you smile, I smile.
When you share, I smile.
When you love, I smile.
When you forgive, I smile.

You want to share your love.
You bring joy to My heart.
I love you so much.

## Let Love Grow

Take time to be still. It is the key to knowing yourself and knowing Me. The stillness opens up the way for My thoughts to be known and heard. Let your mind be still. Let your heart open. Feel the warmth of My presence with you. Take time to connect. Let the warmth of My love fill you. Be still. The stillness of the mind allows the heart to sing. It reaches to your mind in a different way. Allow it to be the center of your thoughts.

The days are filled with so very much. Most of the things don't really matter. What does matter is sharing love. To whom will you give love today?

Love is the strongest power I have given on earth. It has the power to heal wounds. It has the power to melt hearts. It is easily shared, and yet people don't use it as often as they could. Love requires no money. It is an innate feeling that encompasses the essence of who I am. I have placed it within each person. It takes time for people to realize that it is there. Love can melt away negative emotions. It can make a friend. It can draw people together. Love is universal. It doesn't take words. In fact, words can't totally express what love is. It is a feeling but so much more than that. It is the essence of Me placed within each being, no matter how small.

Love does have power that can put Satan in his place. It can embody the truth. It can live and grow within. It can make connections. It can change circumstances. It can unite people.

Love is so needed in the world today. There are people who share love. They realize that by giving it away, there is still a constant supply just like a spring of living water within. They have learned the key to having more is to give it away.

There are those who block love because they don't trust it. It is a sad state of affairs. They won't have more until they give it away. Their negative thoughts squash love, and it stagnates like a water that doesn't move. They can only clean up the water by having it flow again. They are often afraid to trust that love can flow. Out of the heart, love can flow. Allow the heart to open and grow. Let it grow. Let it flow. Let love fill the whole world. I made it that way and need to return to that state. Let it flow.

Let the river of love spread over its banks. It needs to flow freely. Don't be stingy with My love. Don't keep it to yourself. Life is better when there is love flowing freely. People are happier because this love releases chemicals that are healing.

As you praise Me and give Me thanks, those same chemicals rise up within you. They reach Me, and we rejoice together. What a joy I have inside when you take time to praise! It is a delight to know you recognize where love comes from. I am the source of love and all that is good. I prepared this for you. I wanted the world to be connected with Me. That is why I made man in Our image. This was so the love could continue to keep the world alive and filled with the wonder of love.

Don't be so interested in knowing the why of things. Just accept that I made them, and they are good. I put it all together so that it works in unity. When people dwell in unity, I delight in My creation.

There are pockets of love within families. I want to see that spread. If each person would care enough for the stranger in your midst, sharing love and hospitality, you could get back to My intent for creation. Right now, people are isolating. It is not good. People were made to dwell together. Your dwellings and conveniences have kept you apart. A time is coming when you will have to be together and support one another. Prepare your hearts for that time.

My love is not meant to be squelched. It is meant to be bright and caring and fabulously relational. Keep it flowing. Allow it to fill you and to pour out. My love for each person is great. There are times that I cry because My children are in such pain due to their hurts from others. I want people to be loving. I don't mean physical love. I mean caring for the other person in a way that values them and treats them with kindness, filling their need. There are so many people who are wandering away into isolation and not reaching out to others. This hurts all of the people, not just themselves. These people need someone to care enough to love them back into the community, the fold.

As you consider love, remember what it feels like when someone loves you enough to care. Phone calls may help, but there is something more that is needed. It is the physical touch. People need hugs. People need touch because I put it innately within them. It is good to be together. I want people to love with their whole life, giving oneself for another. Forgetting who you are and concentrating on another person is a good thing. Listen to one another. Hear. Really hear what is being said. Take time to affirm one another. Take time to hear the dreams and the hurts so you can support one another. Love without judgment. Only I am the judge. You can never know what the outcome will be, just love.

I know what I am after with love. I am after people who care enough about the other person to uphold them. I know that your hearts are weak unless they are bound to My love. That is why I ask you to center your hearts and open them to Me. I am the way to love because I am love. Be strengthened. Let love shine forth. Allow love to be radiated through all you say and all you do both now and forevermore. Be at peace.

## Love Heals

There isn't a nation where there isn't strife. All over the world healing is needed.

It is not so much that people are broken as they are not in tune with Me. That has to be the first step. They have forgotten Me, just like in the Old Testament. They walk away and become so self-centered. They can only think about themselves, their wants, their desires, their dreams. When they can't get what they want, they become angry. That is often when violence starts because they don't feel heard. It is hard to listen to all the voices and act upon them. It is not something that people can do, but I can. I hear the cries. I hear the frustration. I hear the plans for evil. I hear the cries of the people who deserve justice and don't get it. As I said before, blessed are they who are persecuted for righteousness' sake, for theirs is the kingdom of God. Those who are foolish get what they deserve. However, there are some who truly try to follow Me and are slapped down.

There are those who obey My commandments. I want to help all people learn to follow them. They are ten simple rules that lead to life. Right now, there are many people who are not following them. They are stuck on their own hurts. They want to hurt others because they were hurt. This is not good for mankind. What will really help is for people to be loved and accept that love and forgiveness. They have had generations of hurt, and the ache has built into deep resentment toward others. It must stop. It must stop! It is like a war that is within. It destroys itself and everything it touches. Love is the only thing that combats the hatred. May people understand that people need to be accepted as they are and loved into new behaviors and thoughts. It is only love that can make the change. I am love. I need to be within them. People can help this happen by showing kindness and acceptance. May it be so. Allow this love to grow and be spread.

My Word says that you are to give generously. If someone demands your shirt, give them your cloak also. Help them to know that you care. You may not be in need. They are. They want to have more, be more, be accepted and respected. These are things that they are missing the most. Love, love, love, and more love is needed. Love will conquer all. It will make even the hardest heart melt. May each person reach out in love. It will help the world. It doesn't really matter how many possessions you have. What matters most is that you have love. With that peace will follow.

Know that I am God, and it is My desire that all mankind come to Me. I have the power that can transform. What is needed most is that people come. See that I am good and that I will make a way where there seems to be no way. When My children desire to live in peace, to follow Me, and to be who I made them to be, transformation happens. The world will change. Will you carry the love to make this a reality? I need your love to make a difference.

## Imitate Me

The Bible holds truth. Ephesians 5 shows you how to live in the light, by the Spirit's power.

I have shown you that as My children imitate Me, they live a life filled with love. I showed you how to live this way. Watch the way you talk. Let there be thankfulness to God, not foolish or impure talk. Be honest about your sin so I will be able to grant you forgiveness. Don't hold back from your confession; spill it all. It is the only way I can cleanse you. Do things that are edifying. Don't get pulled into unwholesome talk or actions. Worship only Me.

Carefully determine what pleases Me. Expose the evil, but don't take part in it. Shine My light on it! Darkness can't continue when the light shines in.

Live carefully. Be wise. Make the most of opportunities. Understand what I want you to do. Be filled with the Holy Spirit. Sing psalms, hymns, and spiritual songs. Make music in your hearts that glorifies Me. Thank Me for everything.

Submit to one another out of reverence for Me. Wives—submit to your husbands and respect them. Husbands—love your wives. Be united in marriage as one. All people—feed and care for the body.

These ways of living allow you to have an abundant life. Stay connected to Me. Love big. Love long. Love wide. Love high. Love deeply always as I love you. Amen!

# *Openness*

Have you ever had a memory that seems so clear? It is written in your mind with such detail. It includes feeling, smells, vivid colors, and seems to be happening all over again. This is the power of the mind. There is a lot that the mind holds. Sometimes there is a time when you were all in, living in the present moment. The feelings were high. The time was enjoyable. The joy was full.

There are also times where there is misery. There are memories that you really want to forget, but they are seeped in such depth that it seems impossible to get it out of your mind. The replays of it seem to never end. You try hard to forget, but it seems to just become a deeper hole. These are memories that need to have My healing touch. As you surrender them to Me, I can help them to be less hurtful. Eventually I am able to take out all of the sting as you pay attention to Me.

It was My plan to have everyone be able to think on Me regularly. What has happened in reality is that people are afraid to think about Me. However, when they acknowledge My presence with them throughout the day and night, I lead them to a better way than their own minds can go. I show them the good things. I show them what can be. I show them what is unseen. I put in their minds My will for a situation. It isn't that the way they think is bad, but that My way is better. It is superior because I know all people and the things that I share are from Me. People who are living on earth often only see the physical things that are right before them. I see the spiritual realm.

Opening your heart to the spiritual realm, you must know that I reign on high. There is no issue that I can't take care of. There are so many things that I want to provide, but I don't give to others without agreement. I have so many blessings that people don't even ask for. I have much that I desire to give, but I don't just give it unless I see a willingness on the part of the other person to receive it or to make it work. Man must be open to receive.

Openness requires a gift of the heart. It is riddled with wonder. It doesn't know what is to come. It trusts that whatever it is, I am in it and will provide. Keeping an open heart is important for blessing. However, it can also accept things that aren't of Me, so it is important to know the difference.

Know the truth. Know My ways are steeped in love and light. When there is a dark thought or fear, beware. It is often not from Me. In Me, there is life, truth, hope, and abundant love. Accepting from Me requires hope. Then using what I give requires a step of trust. Be prepared to step out in love when the gift is given. Gifts are meant to be shared, not hoarded or placed on a shelf. Use them. Share them. Bless others with them.

## *Pearl of Great Price*

The pearl of great price is a treasure worth getting. The pearl is something different for each of My children. Consider what it might mean to give all you have to obtain something that is a treasure. That is something worth looking into.

Is the pearl a concept? A way of living? A love for others? A valuable item? Words of wisdom? A person with whom you live? A vast piece of property? A gem? A thing of beauty? Something that will change the world as you know it? Peace on earth? Love abounding? A spring of life overflowing within?

Whatever the pearl is, it is priceless. No amount of money will really get it for you. You have to give your all for it. That would mean giving up the life as you know it to change your ways and go for the pearl. I know that the pearl might seem fleeting, but it is something of worth.

What would be worthy of giving your all? Eternal life? Yes, I give eternal life to those who believe in Me, who are called by name to follow Me. I pray that there will be a hunger for this kind of righteousness that leads to obtaining the pearl of great price. It really has to be given by Me to you. It can't be bought with money. It can only be given by dedication of self to the cause of Christ. It is truly a gift. It is given to those who ask, to those who desire to follow Me. I want to have all people in My kingdom. May people desire to gain this treasure more than anything else. It is indeed one of the greatest treasures that can be obtained. It costs everything. It costs nothing. For the one who believes in Me and wants to live according to My plan, it is free. For the one who lives according to the way of the world, it costs a humble attitude and a change of heart to live in Me. I demand that all who live in love and live in harmony with My teachings, follow Me fully. No detours. No turning back.

## Praise Me

Say to the people, "Let there be praise." Let My praise fill your heart. Let My praises fill the earth! Let there be glory in the land. Let My glory spread for healing of the nations. Let My glory quiet hearts and cause people to repent. Let My glory fill the temples, the churches, the people's hearts. Oh, how I long to do the work to heal all that I made.

Will you praise Me? Will you take time each day to allow My heart and yours to connect? It is My desire. I want us to be in communication. I love My children! I desire to hear from each one every day. Some of My children stay away for years. How it grieves My heart! I love you. Please remember to check in and share your life with Me. I want to show you My love. I want to show you the way I hope for you. I can really only do this in the present. Don't think about what you didn't do in the past or when you might contact Me in the future. Do it now, in the present. Take time at this moment. Put other things aside. Let Me know what is on your heart.

There is so much that I want to give you. However, I have learned that just giving you things doesn't help unless you want it. That is why I want My children to ask. You know how it is with your children. When you know they want something, you seek ways for that to happen. I do that too. My resources are so great. I can give what you haven't even dreamed of. Yet, for you not to ask means that you don't really want it.

Sometimes there are things that you ask for that I know will cause harm. There are things that I know you are not ready to be responsible for. There are things that you don't know how to handle. I hope that you know I will only give you what is best for you. You may request one thing and get another because it is better for you. It may be that you ask for a little, and I give you much or vice versa. I give to you according to your needs. I give to you what I think you will be able to handle.

When things happen that weren't part of My plan for you, I stand even closer than I did before, waiting with you through it. I know that you are more apt to ask in those circumstances, so I am waiting for your request. I know that there are times that I can lift the pain or heal the disease, and I don't choose to do it. Don't take this as a failure. Instead, look for what I am trying to teach you. My faithfulness is there no matter what!

Please remember that I love you. I want to do whatever will be best for you. I want to be first in your life. I want to commune with you. I want to be able to give you good gifts. I want us to have an intimate relationship. These things I long for and continually work to keep in place. I know that there are days that these things are the furthest from your mind. However, I am still near. I wait for you. I long to hear you share thanks and praise. I long to have that praise fill My heart. I long for you to come closer, ever closer. I want to have you sit on My lap and just let Me love you. It is possible in the Spirit.

Let My Holy Spirit lead and guide you to praise. He is always available to you. Do not wait until you are in trouble. Praise especially on good days. The glory of My presence will be evident for all to see. Be filled with joy and let peace lead you forward each day.

# Truth

What is truth? I believe that truth is an absolute. It cannot be changed. It is foundational to all other things. It is something that won't fade away. It is something that one can stand on and know that it won't change.

Truth is built into the inner core of man. That truth is that I exist and that I am the One that makes the universe stay into place. I have captivated the minds and hearts of men when they have considered Me. I am an absolute.

I have made each of My creatures with a truth for them. Each species knows how to follow the pattern. Man is the one creation that I put in the choice to make his or her own decisions. This has caused Me grief since the beginning of time. The choice to live with Me and to live for Me has been something that has kept us at odds for a long time.

The truth is that I long to spend time with My children. I long to satisfy their needs, especially in their inner parts. They so often choose to go their own way, thinking that they know what is best. They don't.

Sometime the truth gets jaded. People make up another story in their minds that seems to explain what is happening. Their egos get in the way other times. They think they can do life on their own. They feel they know how to handle everything. As they go off on their own, some of them do thrive for a while, but that is an external win for them. Internally, they are empty.

My way is not pushy. My way is gentle and mild. I can wait for My children to come back to Me. I put within them a hunger for Me. Some people never realize that hunger. Others do. Oh, that all of My children would realize the need for Me. That absolute truth that I placed within them doesn't go away. It just gets covered up or pushed down by many other things.

My children get themselves in trouble when they refuse to know that truth that only I can satisfy their souls. I am the truth. I am the only one who can satisfy the soul. This truth is the one that people are walking away from. It is such a loss for them and for Me. I long to show them the truth. They don't seem to want it. They don't realize that they have rejected Me. If they did realize this, life could be different. However, man's heart is corrupt when it isn't connected to Me. Having My children return often takes a big issue that they can't handle alone. Oh, how I wish they could return without having to go through that pain. I could save them so much agony if they would be open to sharing their lives with Me on a regular basis.

I am the truth. There are other truths in the world, but this is another interpretation of truth. This truth is more like the rollout of events and what actually happened. This truth is subject to interpretation of the person who sees and experiences it. It is closer to a relative truth because of interpretation. I am absolute truth. That is what really matters. Seek truth. Seek Me.

# *Joy*

Joy fills the heart with sunshine.
It bubbles over in your soul.
It infiltrates the heart with fire
That burns with a heated flame.
It explodes into beauty.
It causes you to rise
To take a step that clicks the heels
And dances in the night.
It lightens hearts.
It brings back youth.
It creates new things in you.
It spills over into kindness,
And helps My work be done.
It brings a smile that dwells within
And never, ever dies,
For I am doing something good
That the heart just can't deny.
Joy brings sweet freshness to the world.
It makes the heart so bold.
It shines like sunshine in your soul,
And makes your life feel whole.

## *This Is the Day*

This day is one I have made. It is a gift to you. Celebrate it! Let My light shine within you as you move through this day.

I so long to direct you. It is because I want to move you closer to Me. I want to help you to be who I made you to be. I have been waiting for you to ask Me for help. I have been waiting for you to agree to fulfill your purpose. If you have it ever before you, you will find that I guide you easily on the path. When you forget your purpose, you wander.

As you keep in contact with Me throughout the day, you will find that the day unfolds with peace, joy, and unity of the Spirit. My Holy Spirit living in you wants a chance to thrive. When you listen to your heart, you will hear Me. I quietly answer your questions and guide you in the way that you should go.

Each day is a masterpiece. You are part of that masterpiece. Your direction is pointing the way for others to be who I made them to be. When you do your part, others come alongside. It works in harmony when people are in touch with My Holy Spirit. When people go off on their own, it takes an unexpected turn, but I am there to guide people back to the path when they are ready.

Yes, there is free choice. That is what happens when people get negative thoughts, when they worry and complain. They become resentful and even sometimes hateful as a result of misunderstandings and hurt feelings. Oh, that My people would quickly deal with offenses and drop them with forgiveness. This would make every day better.

Each day should be filled with wonder. Wonder! Do you wonder what I am doing? I am always at work preparing things for you behind the scenes. I have placed wonder as a part of your mind. Use it for good, not for evil. Make the world a better place as you consider various things. Always strive to leave things better than they were. That way there is agreement about the state of the world.

Each day will be different, unique. As you strive to follow Me, you will find that I enjoy variety. Why else would I have created such diverse people, animals, plants, etc.? I desire for the people who are in touch to make a difference in the world. It is My hope that they listen and work to make changes in the world.

The Father sent Me to make a difference. I helped people to look into their hearts. That is what I hope My followers will do—help people look into their hearts and connect with Me. It is My hope that each person will look into their own hearts each day and get reconnected with Me. I desire to be in constant communion with each one.

What I want is for people to live in the present. They are to enjoy each moment of the day. When things happen that aren't so positive, they need to remember that I work all things together for good—*all* things! Yes! In each day there may be trouble, but I have overcome and will help My followers to do the same. Enjoy the day! Take heart! Live to the fullest! Keep in touch with Me! My love for you is great! Celebrate!

## *Joy in Each Day*

These things that I tell you are from My mind for all of mankind. Share them with others.

Today is the day that I have made. Rejoice! Be glad! Do not come into a new day with dread. Think of all the amazing things that could happen if you opened your mind and heart to what I have prepared. Think about the people that you will see. Think about the amazing ways that I have already created for you to enjoy all around you. Notice the way that I have created each thing uniquely—that includes you! Notice the beauty of the trees, flowers, sky, lakes, and rivers. Listen to the sounds of nature. Listen for My still, small voice.

Each day brings some surprises. Do you notice them? Look for the little things that I bring into your life to bring joy. As you receive some joy, give it away to others. Keep the joy flowing.

It may be a smile, a cup of coffee, a treat, a touch, a compliment, a need, a prayer, whatever! I am in these things, these moments of care. Thank Me for the times that are flowing with joy. Let it continue. Don't let it die with you. Share the joy and it multiplies.

When sorrows come your way, share them too. Find someone who you can share your heart with, even a stranger. It is important to share it, because as you do, it is divided. Someone else is there to help carry the load. Remember that you can share with Me at any time. I am always there as your invisible guide. You can feel Me and know My presence with you. I am always happy when you come to Me and acknowledge that I am with you.

In each day, remember that there will be joys, so look for them. Each day also has trials. These are to make you stronger. When you remember to bring them to Me, you will have My divine help. When you choose to go it alone, your troubles are much heavier. I have told you to bring Me your cares and burdens. What stops you? It doesn't matter how little or how big these burdens are, it is always best to share them.

Some people are too proud to share burdens. They think that it will be too much for someone else. They may think that people will think less of them because they aren't strong enough to deal with these things. However, it is often their stubborn will or pride that holds them back. They might feel embarrassed. They might feel people will talk. Most people are willing to keep a confidence and are honored that you took time to share with them. It is a privilege to receive another's burden. It is even more of an honor to bring it together to Me. This is what I designed for prayer when two or three gather, for I am in their midst.

When you begin to be vulnerable and to share your burdens, you will find that there is joy. It isn't a happy-go-lucky feeling, but there is a depth of joy that wells from the heart. It helps to lighten the situation as it is shared. That is why it divides the heaviness. It brings to light that I am involved and I can do all things.

There are sicknesses that people get that are through no fault of their own. These are difficult to deal with. Sometimes the issue can be solved. Sometimes it cannot. When that happens, I am there to receive the person into My arms and take them to their eternal home.

Each life has its own time frame. While you are living, really live. Don't fret your life away. Live it! When you are giving to others and looking for the good in life, it is exciting! Do what you can while you can. Each day there must be a way to serve Me. Even those who are homebound can find ways to serve Me by writing, calling, connecting with others in ways that can make a difference. Don't give up on spreading joy! It can be found if you take the time to seek it. It can be shared and keep multiplying if you will take the time to reach out to others. Let joy overflow!

## Seek God's Words

Do not worry or fret. I have control. You cannot change a thing by worrying. When you pray about issues and give them to Me without taking them back, I am able to work on the situation. Do your best to stay in the present moment. That is what I give you. Time for Me is eternal. Time for you is measured by days, nights, hours, and minutes. Not so with Me. I see the end from the beginning. I am able to make changes and help people change course when they come to Me. I will not interfere without permission. Do you want what I have for you?

When you stay in My presence, you will find joy. When you wander off on your own, you are unsettled because you don't have direction. I provide an overview, but the day-to-day is up to you. My word never returns to Me void. Therefore, what I tell you will happen with your cooperation. It is when you decide that you have a better idea that things get out of touch. When you worry about things to come instead of looking to Me for each step, you get overwhelmed. You lose your focus and direction.

Think about the things that I have told people through My Word. Find them. Apply them to your life. They are health and healing for your body, mind, and spirit. These promises are for My people. Believe them. Live them. Find the words of the prophets. Apply them. Yes, this means you will need to read the Bible with new eyes. You will need to study as you seek these words. They will be life to you.

Leave behind your cares. Leave behind the old way of doing things. Concentrate on what I am telling you to do. Be made new by the power of the Holy Spirit who lives in you. Listen. Respond. Tell others. It is My way of reaching the earth's people. Follow Me. Will you do it with all your heart, soul, and strength? Will you love Me enough to do what I ask?

Persevere. Do not give up. It is a good path. Keep on the road I have paved for you. Do it with Me and for Me. You won't regret it.

## Joy Comes

Joy like peace can flood your soul. It follows the light and comes when there is a bump of happiness or a constant praise for My glory and delight. It penetrates the spirit then flows through the body bringing wonderful endorphins. Joy is deep.

Joy comes to the Father when His children are obedient, when they look to Him for direction and actually listen, then follow the path of His choosing. The Father's joy is great when His children take time to sit with Him and just be present.

Joy is like a fountain flowing freely. When it is shared, it is contagious. Consider laughter and how when one person keeps laughing, another joins in. Joy is bubbling over causing the belly to shake with laughter. Joy can be hard to contain.

Joy can also be quiet in times of trouble. It is still that understanding that I have your back. That joy can't be diminished and helps you to know that there is no need to worry or fret.

## Joy Explodes

Joy is a feeling that comes from deep within when you know Me. It is something that puts a smile on your heart that ends up on your face. It is joy that makes life exciting. Yes, it is something that bubbles over and makes you want to shout praise to Me on high. Joy is centered on the fact that I am in control of your life and that I am leading you through beautiful times in the spirit.

Yes, you mortals are spirits in a body. The body gets old and wears out, but the spirit, when yielded to Me, just gets more vibrant. That joy that you see in children is circumstantial. Joy in an older person is redemptive. It is energy that is youthful and vivacious. It is centered in My Spirit that lives within.

Joy takes on an energy like fireworks exploding beauty into your life. It excites and lifts. It finds its way to creativity and breaks forth in good deeds that help others. Joy can't be contained. It has to be shared. It rises up and wants to sing hallelujahs!

Joy is My shot of youth and creativity that fills people when they delight in Me. It seeks an outlet. It leads you to dance, to move, to be free to express good vibrations with others. It fills the soul to overflowing.

When I enter a heart, I take full control. I delight in My children's desire to follow Me. I delight in the communication. The more communication we have, the more complete the joy becomes. We can look forward to doing things together as partners.

How I long to partner with you, My child. I want to do great things with you. If you will take time to listen, I will help you find what we are meant to do together. Open your heart and your mind to what can come through joy.

Sometimes I will ask you to go somewhere. Sometimes you may meet someone who needs a word or a touch from Me. Sometimes you will simply praise Me in the midst of joy. I delight in it. Whatever it is that joy brings to your life, receive it and go forth with a grateful, thankful heart for the joy that has been given and expended.

You will live in joy as you go forth in peace knowing that I am the Lord of your life. Gratitude can well up with joy. Thankfulness can spring forth in joy. Kindness can plant more seeds of joy within a heart. As these grow, mature and explode, the world is filled with the joy as well. Don't let joy just sit within you. Share it with the world. Dance, sing, share, create, and let the joy shine forth like a bright light in the darkness. You were meant to share joy. Do it as often as you feel it spring forth. You won't be able to contain it.

## About the Author

Emmanuel Lord is God with us. He desires to be the One we love. He draws people to come to Him. He brings life. His love never ends. He desires to speak with each person and to guide each one into the best way of living. He is always available everywhere.

Sharon Sue Hiller is a spiritual person. She lives with her husband in Rochester, Michigan. She has two married children and five grandchildren. She enjoys singing music that honors God. She is a retired educator, a Stephen minister, and a life coach.